STARS OF POWER
MAGICAL EXPLORATIONS OF THE PENTACLES

T. THORN COYLE

Copyright © 2025 by T. Thorn Coyle
Cover & Book Design © 2025 by T. Thorn Coyle
Editing: Dayle Dermatis

Hardback Edition ISBN: 978-1-946476-61-6

This book, or parts thereof, may not be reproduced in any form without permission, other than what constitutes Fair Use excerpts used for reviews or classroom. Nothing here may be used to train Large Language Models, or GenAI. This book is licensed for your personal enjoyment only.
All rights reserved.

Published by PF Publishing,
An imprint of Triple Flame Inc
3439 SE Hawthorne #203
Portland, OR 97214
Printed and bound by IngramSpark.
Australia: Ingram Content Group AU Pty Ltd, Melbourne, Victoria. US: Lightning Source LLC, La Vergne, Tennessee / Allentown, Pennsylvania / Jackson, Tennessee, United States. UK: Lightning Source UK Ltd, Milton Keynes, United Kingdom. Europe: Lightning Source UK Ltd, with facilities in Germany, France, and Spain.
The authorized representative in the European Economic Area is Lightning Source France, 1 Av. Johannes Gutenberg, 78310 Maurepas, France.
compliance@lightningsource.fr

CONTENTS

Opening   1

PART I: THE ELEMENTS OF LIFE

On a Living Cosmos	5
The Elements	11
Air	15
Fire	18
Water	21
Earth	25
Spirit	29
The Elements and Community	36

PART II: THE IRON AND PEARL PENTACLES

Iron and Pearl   43

THE IRON PENTACLE

Sex	53
Pride	66
Self	79
Power	92
Passion	104
The Cycle Continues	117

THE PEARL PENTACLE

Love	127
Law	139
Knowledge	150
Liberty	161

Wisdom   173
The Cycle Continues   185

PART III: AUTONOMY AND WILL

THE PENTACLE OF AUTONOMY

Commitment   195
Honor   201
Truth   211
Strength   222
Compassion   234
The Cycle Continues   244

Closing   247

And More   251
About the Author   253
Also by T. Thorn Coyle   255

OPENING

At the time of writing this, I have been a student of magic for over forty years.
This book is a deep exploration of some of the core tools I've used for my own self development, including one—the Pentacle of Autonomy—that I crafted myself along the way.

But these tools are not about self development alone.

These pentacles teach us about ourselves, yes, but also about the world. In diligently applying the work held in these pages, we increase our ability to live more centered, balanced lives. We deepen our understanding of the cosmos.

We prepare ourselves to better help this beautiful world. We practice, we make mistakes, and we try again.

Let's dive in....

PART 1: THE ELEMENTS OF LIFE

ON A LIVING COSMOS

Life is made up of disparate parts, sometimes working in harmony, other times discord.

Our relationship to life affects how the world around us affects us, and how we affect the world.

The ancient people all had a direct relationship with the earth and the stars. Many of them were animists, seeing the spark of consciousness within all things. An animist has a very different relationship with the world than a person who sees all things as inert.

Many contemporary Indigenous people are animists, as are some mystics from a variety of cultural backgrounds, along with many who follow Pagan or magical paths. Why is animism important? Because animism reminds us that the cosmos has its own being.

If we treat the cosmos and this planet as living entities, what impact does that have on our individual lives?

First of all, it forces us to recognize that we are not truly individuals, but are parts of a whole, or as I like to say, "We are cells in the body of the cosmos, God Herself." That recognition requires us to make choices about consumption and production, community and friends. If we are part of a larger web, so is every facet of community. Our tiny communities can then reach out in solidarity with other small communities.

The knowledge that I am part of several interlocking interdependent systems changes my entire approach to the world. It enables me to choose my best contributions to the whole.

REGAINING CONNECTION

All children are animists. A child, before their understanding is stunted by social constraints, encounters the world as a living, breathing thing. Stuffed animals become friends. A stick or leaf is a treasure.

To move through the world in this way is to recognize our relationship with the world. We do not master or overcome the world around us, instead, we learn to work with it, and in some cases, establish friendships that can last a lifetime.

A friend once told me a story about people cleaning the kitchen in a Buddhist monastery. One monk admonishes the dishwashers, "Remember, these are the Buddha's bowls!" The sensei, walking by at that moment retorts, "They are not the Buddha's bowls! They are the Buddha's flesh!" This speaks volumes about our relationship to what we consider to be "objects" and to the parts of a theology that says the world is alive, what is divine is immanent, and that everything is sacred.

I've used this story in teaching to illustrate how we treat our "stuff" and why it is that we value a hand-thrown plate more than a factory-made plate. Our animal nature responds to the amount of life force, care, and intention we can sense in the hand-crafted object.

We tend to devalue the factory-made object because we have a harder time relating to it energetically. Yet both are made of similar substances and hold similar patterns. However, a sense of distance from the sacredness of factory-made objects makes it easier to have a "throwaway" culture in which the inexpensive is considered to be disposable—less sacred—than the expensive.

Sometimes expense reflects the amount of labor that went into the making, and other times it is product of some strange status attached to a particular brand. In other cases? The makers are valued less. These humans are considered cogs in a large, exploitive, money-making machine. Because of this, the landfill grows, resources are hoarded even as they dwindle, the earth is ripped apart and the sky polluted.

In the midst of this, we keep buying more, rather than relating more thoroughly to what we already have. These days it is difficult to even get anything repaired. It's cheaper to get a new one. And in some cases, the technology shifts so quickly, the thing needing repair is already outdated. Obsolescence is planned.

So what do we do with that small part of the cosmos? We send it back to China where elderly women and children salvage the various metals, often at great cost to their health.

And how do we acquire something new? Often at devastating cost to children and others mining rare metals in Congo or Sudan, or from people laboring in sweatshops around the globe.

I attended the Parliament of the World's Religions in Melbourne, Australia. There, I had the privilege of meeting two Ainu, the indigenous peoples of Japan. Their practice is pre-Shinto animism, and is reflected in how they relate to the world.

Ainu elder Tsugio Kuzuno spoke of the damage Japan has done to the earth and people by investing so heavily in "growth culture." Living in the US, I certainly understand the perils of constant growth and consumption.

In the midst of his ideas on this, one thing stood out sharply. He said, "...spirits accumulate also in man-made objects. When you make something, you are responsible for what you have made. There is a dark side and a light side to every product. You should not make something that cannot be reabsorbed into nature."

You should not make something that cannot be reabsorbed into nature.

That statement orients us clearly within the sacred, does it not? It implicates our current practices directly in the rending of human relations with the spirit animating this planet, and gives a clear directive for repairing this rupture. The mending begins within, with human attitudes and human ethics. Are we in relationship with the material world or not? My hope is that our answer would be a resounding "yes." But as we look around, it rarely seems to be true.

The second idea that feels germane to this discussion came during the presentation, "The Revival of the European Pagan Traditions." Andras Corban Arthen said that in Gaelic there are two different ways of using the possessive tense, each with its own word. One, which translates as "mine," represents only something that made you or that you made. For example: "my ancestors" or "my child" or "my boat" (if you fashioned the boat) or "my book" (if you wrote the book).

The other possessive form translates as "I am with" to show that you are in relationship with the house or land, or with your partner or colleagues. There is no word for "owning" something that you have not directly made.

This seems like a very helpful distinction. In US terms, I might say that we are in closer relationship with a house that "we own" than one "we rent" because our responsibility to it is greater. But closer relationship still does not connote actual ownership. In reality, no one can or should own land, air, or water. These have their own spirits and should be shared for the common good.

We can tie this back to Kuzuno's thoughts on responsibility for things we have made—if Dell or Apple computers says "these are our computers" in the first possessive usage, they are taking responsibility along with ownership. Not only can they claim credit for the benefits that their computers give, but they can also claim responsibility for the toxic waste that is the end product, and by extension, the health of workers mining the rare metals and creating the computers, as well as those affected by the salvage of parts.

Ainu leader Ryoko Foose told us that in their language, the name given to Mother Earth reflected the relationship between her and humans. If true relationship to the sacred in all things was consistently recognized, how might the climate talks go differently? Would Walmart even be in business, were there not a flood of inexpensive (cheap in labor cost, but high in cost to humans and environment) and highly disposable goods available? How about Amazon? How about every fast-fashion manufacturer?

I look around at my home filled with objects. Most of it consists of books and handmade art collected over decades, all things that are pleasing to my soul. Yet I also acknowledge that if I had fewer of these beautiful objects, my relationships to each might feel more intimate. I might come to know them better.

They are all the Buddha's flesh. They, and we, are all part of the unfolding cosmos.

Each day, how do we try to remember the sacred? How can we tune our lives to come into closer and more healthy relationships with everything: animate or inanimate, animal, vegetable, mineral, water, fire, soil, or flesh? Paint, ceramic, or petroleum, plastic, chemical or quark?

And how might society change when we do?

Practice:

Examine your relationship with the world around you. Are there trees? Desert plants? Sun? Rivers? Snow? Ocean? City buildings? Animals? Humans? How do you relate or avoid any or all of these? What is one thing you could do to shift one of these relationships in a way that feels healthy and satisfying?

Now examine your relationship to things in your life. Art. Books. Cookware. Electronics. Cars. Camping gear. Clothing. Shoes. Food. Are there things you could take better care of? Are there things you could show deeper appreciation of? Are there things that you could pass along to someone else, or let go of? Are there things you could repair?

THE ELEMENTS

To speak of the Elements of Life is to also speak of relationship.

The ancient Babylonians honored sea, earth, sky, and wind. The Chinese traditions honor fire, water, wood, metal, and earth. Ancient and contemporary Hindus look to æther, air, fire, water, and earth. The Ancient Greeks later adopted this same system. Alchemists followed this tradition, also working with air, fire, water, earth, and æther, and this passed down to practitioners of contemporary magic and Paganism.

Occasionally, æther is also known as the void, and later traditions often call this spirit. The void, the Great Zero, is the place where things arise and return. Spirit is that which imbues and animates all living things.

Æther is also the repository of all knowledge and connection, enabling the mystic and magician to access different realms of consciousness.

To honor the elements is to orient ourselves with this planet, the cosmos, and our own interior landscapes. We comprehend that the elements of air, fire, water, and earth are simple stand-ins for the rich variety of the elements that make up our cosmos. My animal nature understands the simplicity of five elements. I use them as a starting point to open a conversation with the world.

Invoking the base elements is the task of the magic worker, the Pagan, the animist, and the witch.

As for the void? The zero? The cosmic egg? The numinous and ineffable? To invoke æther is to call in possibility and mystery. Invoking mystery is the task of practitioners of all sorts of spiritual paths. It is the task of the mystic and the seer, as well as individuals and communities desiring to weave a sense of the sacred more tightly into their lives.

To acknowledge æther is to recognize that, while our rational minds may not comprehend them, there are many realms around us, seen and unseen. Through spiritual practice or moments of epiphany or trauma, we can encounter these realms.

When we invoke spirit, we invoke the unknown, and acknowledge that which is unknown within the cosmos, each other, and ourselves.

THE SEASONS OF LIFE

We all have an affinity for different elements. Some of us will be drawn toward water, and some to earth, air, or fire. Still others enjoy spending most of their time in spirit or aether.

Are you more emotionally based, physically based,

mentally based, or energy based? Those are keys to your primary elemental affinity.

But that said, no one person is attracted only to or centered in one of the classical elements. We're all a mixture, and that is part of what keeps us healthy and balanced, and able to enjoy many facets of life.

Also, during various phases of our lives, we may shift elemental affinity. We may have seasons of fire and seasons of earth. For some of us, this will literally map to the yearly seasons around us. For example, I manifest much more fire and air during spring through summer. The earlier the sun rises, the earlier my brain wakes up. I use this more fiery time to do the bulk of my generative work and therefore get a lot of writing done! Autumn into winter, I have greater access to earth and water mode, engaging in more contemplation and working on earthy, business-related tasks.

Does this mean I do no writing during winter and no business tasks during summer? No. I just know where my strengths lie during those times and adjust my schedule to reflect that.

I have friends who are opposite. Winter is their generative time. How about you?

It is useful to begin to track what elements are strongest for us during certain months of the year. We can adjust activity and rituals in accordance with these personal cycles.

There are also larger elemental cycles tied to life events, circumstances, and the aging process. These, too, will look and feel different for each of us. My forties, for example, were a time of fire and earth, with a whole lot of spirit running through it all. My fifties have largely been a time of earth and water and a shifting relationship with air and fire as my writing business grows and my relationships to body and home grow richer and more nuanced.

Through all these phases, my spiritual practice has shifted and changed, and I'm now in a new phase of deepening and expansion.

ACTION:

Map your year according to which elements you suspect are strongest during the various physical seasons. Double check when you are in the midst of each season and reflect on whether your assumption feels accurate in real time.

Now look at the seasons of your life. Which elements felt strongest during your teens? What elements came into play around early or later adulthood? What element comes to the forefront when you shift careers or jobs? When you engage in activism or the arts? When illness comes knocking?

How are you making choices to engage with life? What elements do you draw upon? Which elements need more support?

AIR

The power of Air is the power of mind and of breath.

Imagine yourself standing on a clifftop, being buffeted by wind. How do you respond? Do you fight against the push of air? Do you allow yourself to move, dancing with its power?

Close your eyes. Take a breath and still yourself as much as you can.

Imagine that the great wind cleanses the energy fields around you, sweeping away worry, shame, and strife. Inhale. Fill with life. Pause. Exhale. Connect with everything that lives.

CHART YOUR MIND

What thoughts do you have upon waking?
What thoughts arise during meditation?
Are there phrases you habitually return to?
Are there thoughts you actively avoid?

Beginning to chart our thought patterns is key to self-knowledge.

CHART YOUR BREATH

Begin to notice how often your breathing feels constricted. Where is it constricted? Your throat? Your diaphragm? Lower in your belly?

Notice when your breathing feels loose and as if you can fully fill your lungs.

What causes either situation? Just notice.

CONNECTING WITH AIR

Connecting with the Powers of Air help us with discernment and presence. Magic begins with breath. The mind helps us assess information coming from our emotions, our bodies, and our surroundings. The mind parses the onslaught of input from computers, television, and world events.

If we cannot learn to know our own minds, we are forever at the mercy of outside influences. We can hone our critical thinking skills. We can retrain our mental habits over time via prayer, meditation, reading challenging articles or books, engaging in discussions about concepts, or dissecting events from a distance.

Over time, when a thought arises, we will recognize it and be able to choose how to respond, rather than responding by default. The same will be true of our emotions, but we'll get to that later.

Lack of critical thinking and discernment trips us up as

individuals and collectively. We become reactionary instead of acting from a grounded, centered place. We respond to a constant bombardment of stimuli and information, trying to deflect or keep up, our emotions and thoughts manipulated and overwhelmed by the sheer constancy of input.

The longer we are rooted in reaction, the less able we are to form accurate opinions, let alone strategize clearly.

When we have a clearer relationship with our thought patterns, we can also set clear intentions.

Slowing our breathing down and taking time to center is the first step to developing a healthier relationship with the Power of Air.

FIRE

The power of fire is the power of will, synapse, and energy.

Imagine yourself standing in front of a roaring bonfire. How do you respond? Do you wince away from the heat and smoke? Do you lean in? Do you break into a feral grin, reveling in the fire's power?

Close your eyes. Still yourself as much as you can. Feel the vitality and warmth of sun, of spark, of arc, of fire....

Imagine that fire warming you, enlivening you, filling you with light and energy. Feel the fire. Inhale. Fill with life. Pause. Exhale.

CHART YOUR RELATIONSHIP TO FIRE

What is your relationship to sunlight and warmth?

Do you cook over fire? Electricity? Do you light candles?

Do you have enough energy to get through the day?

Do you allow yourself to experience passion? Does this feel enlivening, or are you overtaken by your passions?

Are there energetic patterns you actively avoid?

Beginning to chart our energy patterns is key to developing our will.

CHART YOUR ENERGY

Are you currently jittery, sluggish, or easily overwhelmed? Are you quick to move, or slow?

What are your energy levels upon waking?

Begin to notice how often your energy feels constricted. Where is it constricted? Your diaphragm? Lower in your belly? You sex? Your limbs?

When does your energy feel drained? How does this affect you?

Notice when your energy feels strong and loose and as if you can channel that energy where you need it.

What causes any of these situations? Just notice.

CONNECTING WITH FIRE

Connecting with the Powers of Fire help us with will and action. Magic flows on energy. Without a strong energetic flow, it is hard to sustain activity and apply our intentions.

Our energy levels are a good indicator of overall life balance and health. If our energy is consistently feeling drained, or eaten instead of fed, that's a sign that we need to shift some habits and patterns.

Are we consistently throwing our energy away? Do we need

more exercise or less? More sleep? Different food sources? Do we need to step away from people or projects that drain or eat our energy, or can we find a healthier-for-us relationship with those people or projects?

And what about will? Will is the ability to set intention into action. Does our will feel strong? Weak? Unfocused? Do we tense up in order to get anything done? Are we avoiding our desires? Are our wants and needs met?

Are we able to follow through with intentions or promises?

What does it feel like to actively pursue our wants, needs, and desires? What does it feel like to avoid them?

Accurately gauging our energy levels and our relationship to will helps us develop a stronger relationship with the Power of Fire.

WATER

The power of water is the power of flow, emotion, and dreams.

Imagine yourself standing in front of an ocean, a pond, or a flowing stream. How do you respond? Do you wish to immerse yourself? Do the depths feel frightening? Do you long to touch the ebb and flow, charting a new course within the water?

Close your eyes. Still yourself as much as you can. Feel the coolness, the ripples, the currents as they tug at you, body, mind, and soul....

Imagine that water filling you, quenching you, filling you with the moisture you so desperately need. Feel clear, clean water. Cup your hands and drink it in. Fill with life. Pause. Exhale. Connect with the water within and around you.

CHART YOUR RELATIONSHIP TO WATER

What is your relationship to water and flow?

How much water do you drink throughout the day?

How often do you shower or bathe, wash your face or brush your teeth?

How often do you experience water? How about your dreams? Your psychic awareness?

Do you allow yourself to experience your dreams? Do you seek out the hidden depths in your psyche or soul, or do you avoid them?

Beginning to chart our emotional patterns is key to developing emotional strength and resilience.

CHART YOUR EMOTIONS

Are you currently joyful, in love, fearful, constricted, or expansive?

What is your emotional state upon waking? How about at the end of each day?

Begin to notice how often your emotions feel constricted or suppressed. Where are they constricted? Your heart? Your belly? Your throat? Somewhere else?

When do your emotions feel distant or hard to reach? How does this affect you?

When does emotion feel overwhelming? Do you know why?

Notice when your emotional state feels steady, and with good boundaries. Notice how often you feel in the flow.

What causes any of these situations? And what is the result? Just notice.

CONNECTING WITH WATER

Connecting with the Powers of Water help us with heart, intuition, and emotions. It is often said that our psychic impulses are amplified by water and affected by emotion. Cultivating our relationship with water helps us deepen our relationship with our personal subconscious, which gives rise to creativity and intuition.

Like our energetic states, our emotional states are a good indicator of overall life balance and health. If our emotions are constantly suppressed or turned up too loud, we may need to shift our patterns. For some of us, this means engaging with the body in order to tap our emotions. In my life, dance enabled me to open more fully to emotion. For others, this might mean therapy or making a commitment to share more with close friends.

Are we consistently blocking our sense of flow? Do our emotions run amok or get locked under tight control? How does food, sleep, exercise, work, or play affect our emotional states and our sense of flow?

Do we need to set clearer boundaries? Do we need to honor our emotions instead of discounting them? Or do we need to train our emotions to work with the rest of our lives instead of taking over and drowning what we really need?

And what about our hearts? Our physical heart regulates the flow of blood throughout our body. Our metaphysical heart enables us to develop courage and daring and the ability to take risks to expand our lives beyond the current perimeters set by ourselves or those around us.

Are we willing to take the risk to open our hearts and tap the flow of magic in our lives?

What might it feel like to open to our dreams and to trust our intuition? What might we become if we engaged our emotions and opened to the greater flow?

Accurately assessing our emotions and our relationship to intuition and flow helps us develop a stronger relationship with the Power of Water.

EARTH

The power of earth is the power of nature, body, and wealth.

Imagine yourself standing on a mountain, in a forest, a desert, or a city park. How do you respond? Do you long to touch the ground? Does connecting with the natural world feel sustaining? Do you feel safe here, or anxious? Do you feel rooted, grounded, or uncertain? Do you wish to escape this place, or stay?

Close your eyes. Still yourself as much as you can. Feel the solidity of the earth beneath you, hear the sounds of birds or animals. Feel your own body, in this place and time....

Imagine that earth can support you and sustain you. Imagine being cradled, nurtured, and filled with strength. Feel structure that lends stability, rather than structure that feels like a cage. Feel the living nature of earth. Pause. Exhale. Connect with your body, your skeleton, your muscles. Feel all the ways in which you are one with earth.

CHART YOUR RELATIONSHIP TO EARTH

What is your relationship to earth?

What sort of foods do you regularly eat? Do you enjoy them? Do they feel nourishing?

How often do you move your body, stretching tense muscles, or building strength?

How often do you experience earth? How about your relationship to home? Your ability to provide sustenance and structure?

Do you allow yourself to experience the possibility of health and prosperity? Do you have the ability to share resources with others? What is your relationship to the gifts of earth?

Beginning to chart our physical patterns is key to developing true strength and flexibility.

CHART YOUR PHYSICALITY

Do you currently feel strong or weak? Flexible or inflexible?

What does your body feel like upon waking? How about at the end of each day?

Begin to notice how often your muscles feel constricted, or tired, or overworked. Where are they constricted? How often are they tired or overworked? Do you know why?

What are your physical pain levels? Or fatigue? How does this affect you?

When does physical reality feel overwhelming? Do you know why?

Notice when your body, home, and relationship to

resources (including money) feel stable, strong, and on course. Notice what feels out of alignment.

What causes any of these situations? And what is the result? Just notice.

CONNECTING WITH EARTH

Connecting with the Powers of Earth helps us with health, manifestation, and wealth. A strong connection to the land around us strengthens our connection to our personal physical realms. Cultivating our relationship with earth helps us deepen our relationship with the shifts in our bodies, our work, and our generosity.

Like our energetic and emotional states, our connection to the physical is an indicator of overall life balance and health. If our bodies constantly feel battered or neglected, we may need to shift our patterns. For some of us, this means engaging with different forms of exercise or stretching, or shifting our eating. In my own life, my relationship with food, exercise, and sleep have all shifted over the years, especially as I've come to understand a chronic health issue. For others of us, this shift may mean more rest or more challenging physical activity, or releasing an attachment to certain kinds of eating, or allowing ourselves to welcome more physical pleasure in our lives.

Are we consistently avoiding what might help us feel more physically present? Do we need to shift our attitude toward work, money, or resources? How do food, sleep, exercise, work, or play affect our physical states and our sense of stability and strength?

Do we need to throw out old thought forms around the

physical? Do we need to hold up a different mirror, or throw out mirrors altogether? Or do we need to go outside more, spend time away from phones or computers? Listen to our bodies and the land?

And what about the things we build and build upon? Our skeletons and muscles carry us around. Our bodies make beds, till soil, caress a beloved's face, dance, make art, and sing.

And other times? Our bodies rest in silence.

What might it feel like to allow ourselves to simply be? To enjoy our bodies as they are? To feel gratitude for what we have? To notice the things we can share?

What do you take for granted in the physical realms of nature, work, home, money, and loved ones? How might you change that?

Accurately assessing our physical reality and our relationship to flexibility and stability helps us develop a stronger relationship with the Power of Earth.

SPIRIT

The power of spirit or aether is the power of the numinous, the ineffable, the imagination, and a sense of pure connection.

Imagine yourself. Feel yourself. Notice your emotions, your body, your thoughts…. Now take a breath and drop into your center. Imagine yourself in a place of stillness. Quiet. Serenity.

Breathe here for a while.

Now imagine that stillness slowly filling itself with swirling light or soft clouds. Imagine your own self growing lighter, more luminous, and more expansive. Allow your edges to soften. Allow your mind to expand.

Keep breathing. Keep softening and allowing yourself, not to reach, but to flow outward from your center, seeking a space outside space, and a time outside time.

Feel distant stars. Sense past and future. Sense all who have come before and all who are yet to be. Sense those beings who move between the seen and unseen.

Return to center. How do you feel, imagining all of this? Does it feel enlivening and intriguing? Does it feel confusing, or fill you with uncertainty? Does it make you want to escape your life as it is, or to connect more fully with all that is?

Close your eyes. Still yourself as much as you can. Feel your breath. Sense your heartbeat. Notice the edges of your skin and the energy fields around you. Imagine you reside within an egg of light and know that this light is also you. No separation.

Fill with this sense of light and connection. Feel the ways in which you have a boundary and are boundless.

Inhale. Connect with life. Exhale. Connect with spirit.

In this space, within this connection, there is nothing you cannot be.

CHART YOUR RELATIONSHIP TO SPIRIT

What is your relationship to spirit?

How often do you check in with those who came before you, whether they are connections of blood or spirit?

How often do you allow yourself to slow down and simply be?

How often do you sit in contemplation or meditation? How often do you light a candle and speak a prayer?

How often do you experience spirit? How about your relationship to creativity? Your wish to tap into a flow that is larger than yourself?

Do you allow yourself to experience the possibility of expansion? Do you cultivate a trust in your intuition or other psychic skills? What is your relationship to the gifts of spirit?

Beginning to chart our spiritual patterns is key to centering, imagining, and being.

CHART YOUR SPIRITUAL NATURE

Do you currently feel present or scattered? Calm, shut down, or agitated?

What is your attitude upon waking? How about at the end of each day?

Begin to notice how often you feel as if you are not truly present in your life. How much do you live in the past or worry about the future? How often are you in escapism mode? Do you know why?

What are your psychic pain levels? Is your intuition shut down, or open? How does this affect you?

How often do you connect with your spiritual side? How strong does that connection feel? How regular or erratic is your spiritual practice?

Notice when your spirit feels centered. Notice what feels out of alignment. Notice the effect that things like yoga, meditation, prayer, spell work, or altar building have on your attitude and your life.

What is the result of an absent spiritual practice? What is the result of an active spiritual practice? Just notice.

CONNECTING WITH SPIRIT

Connecting with the Powers of Aether helps us with equanimity, possibility, and imagination. A strong connection to spirit strengthens our connection to our creativity, curiosity, and sense of well-being. Cultivating our relationship with spirit helps us deepen our relationship with the shifts in all aspects of our lives.

Like our energetic, physical, and emotional states, our connection to the spiritual is an indicator of overall harmony or disharmony. If our spirit constantly feels squashed, beleaguered, or attacked, we may need to shift our patterns to shore up our internal strength. For some of us, this means engaging with different forms of spiritual reading or practice. In my own life, my relationship with prayer and meditation changed after my brain injury. I needed to access different systems of support in order to return to a practice that felt sustaining. I used things like binaural beats and timed sessions to help me.

For others of us, this shift may mean more time in front of our altars, or to add in something like walking meditation, or doing centering practice both in the morning and before we go to bed. I find that bracketing my day with spiritual practice as my first and final acts to be very beneficial.

QUESTION:

Are we consistently avoiding what might help us feel more spiritually centered? Do we need to shift our attitude toward cultivating intuition, or spending time in ritual? How does our attention to our spiritual and psychic well-being affect our physical, emotional, mental, and creative health? How does attention—or lack thereof—to our spiritual and psychic well-being affect our relationships?

Do we need to refresh our commitments to spiritual or

psychic practice? Do we need to spend more time on the meditation cushion, or communing with the trees?

And what about expansion? Have our lives become too small, or too scattered? Do we need to gather our energies or enter into the larger flow of the cosmos?

What helps to free your spirit? Is that music, dance, art, nature, prayer, song, love, laughter? What helps you share your spirit with others?

What will you commit to this week?

Accurately assessing our spiritual reality and our relationship to the seen and unseen helps us develop a stronger relationship with the Power of Spirit.

COLLECTIVE THOUGHT, ACTION, AND EMOTION

Every collective can intentionally build a group mind. This group mind grows into a collective consciousness, storing group patterns and knowledge. This collective consciousness, with time and feeding, can also become the group spirit.

But we also form these collective entities inadvertently, as well, creating patterns, mores, protocols, and unspoken contracts or agreements.

You can think of this in simpler terms of what poet Robert Bly called "the third body." The third body arises from the relationship between two people. There is one individual, and a second individual, and the two together form yet another being. Any relationship has this third body, a being that forms its own patterns, and carries its own energetic and emotional signatures. The more intimate a relationship becomes, the stronger the patterns of that third body also become.

The third body can help make us braver than we are while alone, and the third body can also drag us into conformity. Now, extrapolate this out to families, communities, magical groups, and cultures, and you can begin to see the power and impact of the group mind and group spirit.

A group spirit can be as simple as the joy formed by a group of friends at their weekly game night. Or this third body can be made by three people getting together to write, or twenty people sitting in meditation together. This is easy to measure by reading the effects of these gatherings. Do you write more when you are around others? Is meditation or prayer easier to access when others around you are doing the same?

By consciously feeding what we want into the group mind, we help the clarity of our groups and can better uphold the mission we collectively hold.

A mission statement is a spell to invoke a group spirit and ethos. How many times are mission statements forgotten or actively undermined? That has an effect on the group mind and begins to distort group action.

We want to be as conscious as possible about what we are creating together, and how.

Even social media sites form their own beings, chaotic as they may seem. This is why I try my best to put out signal rather than noise into the æthers. The more I contribute to noise, through unconscious reaction usually, the more fractured and fractious the group mind becomes.

Self feeds community and community feeds self. And that is true of our words and thoughts as well as our actions.

Group spirits can encompass many of the classical elements: they can grow from emotions, actions, and will. But I wanted to write about them as they relate to air, because shifting these beings can most easily begin with the mind. We can set an intention toward change and steer the group mind from there.

As we move through the other elements, notice how some of the material and work relates to this third body and the thought-forms we build. How are these beings affected by emotions, for example? And what happens when they are fed or starved of energy?

THE ELEMENTS AND COMMUNITY

Sometimes it is helpful to assess what is happening with the elements vis-à-vis our communities. This could mean examining balance and imbalance in our households, workplace, schools, temples, covens, activist groups, or any other consistent group.

What is the elemental mix in the group? What helps strengthen the group? What offers inspiration or hope? What helps the group develop flexibility? What helps a group grow?

Conversely: What destabilizes the group? What undermines its foundations or washes them away? What increases conflict? What diffuses purpose?

I could list dozens of ways we can assess how the elements are impacting our relationships, but instead of reading through lists, it is far better that we center ourselves and pay attention to the elements at work around us.

Below are some questions we can ask ourselves as we learn

to use elemental assessment as a tool for community health and well-being.

AIR

How do we share ideas? How are fresh ideas welcomed and fostered? Are we limiting fresh ideas? How often do we simply breathe together? In meetings or conversations, who talks the most? Who listens? Can we find better ways to make space for both speaking and listening? Do we study together? What are we learning and how? Do we welcome air by singing together? Playing music? Sharing poetry? Does our group honor mental health and brain function differences? How do we welcome air? How do we offer each other space to breathe?

FIRE

What is our overall energy level? Are we interested and engaged with each other and/or our project? Are there people who always work to boost energy levels and engagement? Are there clusters who drag our energy down or drain the group? How often do we take breaks together to just have fun? How much leeway is there to refuel ourselves and each other? Do we need to get back to basics in order to feed the fire? Or do we need to add something new, to increase the warmth? How can we better welcome varied expressions of energy and find a place for them to be?

WATER

How often does our household or community feel in the flow? What sorts of activities increase our sense of flow? What blocks the flow? How do we make space for emotions in our group? Do we laugh together? Cry? Can we be intense? Angry? Does one person's emotions supersede everyone else's needs? Are emotions squashed or frowned upon? Do people overall feel satisfied or happy? Is stress or fear our main motivator? How can we increase a sense of ease and emotional health?

EARTH

What are the practical building blocks of our household, group, or community? How often or how well do we tend them? Do we share the work of making food or repairing structures? Organizing activities? Keeping track of each other's physical well-being? Keeping our tasks on track? Or do one or two people always end up taking on the bulk of the work? How often do we engage in physical activity together? Do we allow ourselves and each other to tend to our physical needs and overall health? How accessible is our group to physical differences? How can we better encourage sharing labor and taking care of ourselves?

SPIRIT

When we examine group dynamics, what do we notice? How often do we revisit our core mission or our key assumptions? What is the spirit of our household, group, or community? How would we describe our group? Is there room to grow or change? If we were to start over tomorrow, how would we want to shape our group? What might we add or take away? Does our personal spirit align with the spirit of the community or household? What causes a sense of misalignment? What methods do we share to increase an overall sense of continuity, inclusion, or purpose? What are our hopes and collective dreams?

IN WORKING with the elements in community, our attention opens to many things we may not otherwise observe, including our own reactions to situations, conversations, or work tasks Our animal natures pick up on subtle and subconscious cues that our personalities don't always recognize. Taking a few moments at the start or end of a week to run through a basic elemental assessment can awaken us to noticing more and also noticing more quickly. If we train ourselves and encourage each other to look at the world this way, we may come to notice imbalances in the moment, increasing our capacity to shift in real time. Even if we aren't in a position to share this work with others directly, doing this practice ourselves might help us speak up more in meetings, or have concise, clear feedback to offer.

"I noticed Jessie ends up taking on all the organizational tasks, which means they don't have as much room to contribute this other awesome skill." Or, "Robin, you always deal with the recycling every week. Is that still okay with you, or should we switch that up?" Or, "I notice a lot of tension in the room right now. Is there something we need to address?"

Elemental assessment is just another tool. It doesn't need to be a big deal. As a matter of fact, the simpler and easier we allow it to become, the more effectively it can work to increase our personal and community health and function.

PART II: THE IRON AND PEARL PENTACLES

The Iron and Pearl Pentacles are magical tools that came through witch, teacher, and mystic, Victor H. Anderson.

I was introduced to the Iron Pentacle when I was eighteen. The Feri Tradition teacher I was with at the time mostly had us run the energies through our bodies to rebalance the points of Sex, Pride, Self, Power, and Passion inside ourselves and, hopefully, our lives.

I broke my training with that teacher for a variety of reasons—mostly ethical—and moved on.

The second time I was introduced to the Iron Pentacle was via the Reclaiming Collective—now the Reclaiming Tradition. We worked each point intensely, one at a time, and examined how they flowed together, or were blocked, or working at cross purposes in our lives.

I also studied Pearl Pentacle at that time, one of the teachers, Pandora Minerva O'Mallory, remarked that Iron was the work of a lifetime, and Pearl was the work of many lifetimes.

It was then I realized working the Iron Pentacle was revolutionary, and that Pearl was evolutionary. That Iron was the work of my lifetime, and Pearl was the work of our lives, collectively.

I studied, and eventually began to teach Iron and Pearl, and continued to work these powerful tools in my own life, while passing them along to students, colleagues, and peers.

The next time I encountered Iron and Pearl was via the very witch they emerged through: Victor H. Anderson. Studying with him further refined my understanding of the tools and helped to focus my work.

I have been forever changed by these tools. I firmly believe that a person who engages with an open heart and curious mind, ready to face themselves and the world, will find great gifts of insight and burgeoning wisdom. These gifts of insight hold the power to change how we come to know ourselves and each other.

The better we know ourselves, the better we come to know the world around us, and vice versa.

We open our potential to live as fully functional human beings, not shells or projections of humanity.

We connect with the elements of life, with magic, with science, with poetry, with art. We learn to better work with each other in community and solidarity.

Through this work—within ourselves and with each other—we can co-create a kinder, more just world.

DOING THE WORK

The work of the Iron and Pearl Pentacles is both a form of magic and self-development, though that latter gets a bad name in some magical circles.

Self-development can be navel gazing or solipsistic but doesn't have to be. The more we know ourselves, the better able we are to work in community. And the more we work in community, the more our self is reflected and refined.

Life is a constant dance with other beings, and so is magic.

The work of the Iron and Pearl Pentacles is magic because these concepts and energies are transformative. They adjust the way energy flows in our subtle bodies and enable us to open to greater and greater energy flow over time.

Magic works on these energies.

PART II: THE IRON AND PEARL PENTACLES

These pentacles are self-development for similar reasons. They fine tune our strengths and show us our weaknesses. We can both invoke—call in—and evoke—call forth—these energies to alter our lives.

These tools also teach us how to track the flow of energy in society and the world around us. For example, it has been said that what I have named the overculture runs these energies anticlockwise around the outer circle:

Sex, or life energy, flows toward Power, which flows toward Pride, which flows toward Passion, which flows toward Self. This can distort the flow, amplifying unhealthy aspects of each point, bringing people and organizations further and further out of alignment. This anticlockwise wheel bolsters Power-Over rather than what Starhawk and others have called Power from Within and Power With.

To truly engage with the Iron and Pearl Pentacles is to work toward liberation for others and within ourselves.

These practices are what led me to develop a new pentacle, which I sometimes name the Pentacle of Autonomy. I'll talk about that later in this book.

The freer we are, the less under the influence of harmful outside forces we become, the more our creativity and courage blossom, and the better able we are to help one another through life, and toward justice.

THE IRON PENTACLE

There is iron in every star. As a supernova explodes, it releases that iron, spreading those atoms throughout the solar system. These heavy atoms disperse, and gravity helps shape them into new forms.

It is said that there is iron at the heart of planet Earth. Red, and molten, some say. Earth is rich in iron, and—for good or ill—iron has become a key building block to many human civilizations over time.

There is iron in our blood, that connects us back to the stars.

For me, the iron within us, and the star shape of my four limbs and head reminds me of this resonance. We are one with our cosmos, not separate from it. This cosmos is our home.

The iron in our blood helps carry oxygen through our bodies, keeping us alive. We ingest this iron through the food we eat. In this way, iron also reminds us that we are of this planet, just as this planet is of the stars.

And so, we are brought to the first point on the Iron Pentacle, to Sex. To the stuff of life itself. The rest of the Iron Pentacle flows from this.

To invoke iron is to invoke life. To invoke iron is to invoke health. To invoke iron is to invoke connection.

No human being can live in a vacuum. Without connection, we die. Whether that connection comes via the air we breathe, generated by plants and trees, or the food we eat, or the people we befriend, as long as we are on this planet, we are never alone.

Iron reminds us of this. We have a place here, in this cosmos. Let us claim that place.

PART II: THE IRON AND PEARL PENTACLES

INVOKING IRON

We invoke the power of the iron in our blood. We invoke the fire at the core of the earth. We invoke our humanity.

We invoke the power of Sex, of life force, and creativity.

We invoke the power of Pride, of knowing our place in the world.

We invoke the power of Self, of knowing all our parts.

We invoke the power of Power, of comprehending our ability to act and do.

We invoke the power of Passion, fostering deep engagement and desire.

We invoke the Pentacle of Iron.

Practice:

Note: if you live in the Southern Hemisphere and feel more comfortable shifting this so clockwise and anticlockwise are correct for you, please feel free.

Stand or lie down, with enough room to arrange your arms and legs into a star position. If your body is not able to do this, get as comfortable as possible, and know that you can run energy both through your physical body and toward a star shape around your physical body.

If you are standing, you can lower your arms whenever you need to, and raise them again as you have the energy or strength to do so.

Let us begin.

Slow your breathing down. Connect with your center, that

place of stillness between your navel and your pelvis. Breathe into center.

Now, imagine the fire at the molten iron core at the center of the earth. Breathe. Now, imagine the fire and iron in the distant stars. Breathe.

As you inhale, draw up iron from the earth, and fill your body with that energy. As you exhale, connect with the iron in the distant stars. Repeat this until you've established a rhythm and a connection: heart of the earth, center of your body, heart of the stars, return. Heart of the earth, center of your body, heart of the stars, return. Heart of the earth, center of your body, heart of the stars, return.

Now, imagine that red iron energy forming itself into a small ball inside your head, somewhere behind your third eye or pineal gland.

Feel it glowing there. Name that point Sex.

Now, imagine that red iron energy flowing down your body, forming a small ball in your right foot.

Feel it glowing there. Name that point Pride.

Now, imagine that red iron energy flowing up your body, forming a small ball in your left hand.

Feel it glowing there. Name that point Self.

Now, imagine that red iron energy flowing across your body, forming a small ball in your right hand.

Feel it glowing there. Name that point Power.

Now, imagine that red iron energy flowing down your body, forming a small ball in your left foot.

Feel it glowing there. Name that point Passion.

Now, imagine that red iron energy flowing back up your body, back to the small ball in your head. Name that point Sex.

PART II: THE IRON AND PEARL PENTACLES

Pause a moment here and breathe awhile. Notice all the points: Sex, Pride, Self, Power, Passion. Notice how your energy forms a star.

Keep connecting with, and relaxing into, your breath.

Now, imagine a clockwise circle being traced around your body, from Sex, to Self, to Passion, to Pride, to Power, and back to Sex.

Keep breathing. Notice how you feel. Notice the possibility in this form. Your form. Your life.

Are you ready to continue?

SEX

The Iron Pentacle begins and ends with Sex, because sex is the stuff of life itself.

To begin any conversation about the sex point must include a discussion of life force. Raw energy. The stuff that makes trees root more deeply into the earth, and bees to flit flower to flower.

Sex is a form of energetic and physical connection. Sex includes pleasure in its many forms. Generative creativity is another aspect of the Sex point.

Can asexual people have a relationship to sex? Of course. Asexual people can experience physical pleasure of all kinds, including through what we might ordinarily call sexual activity. And creativity is not the purview of any one type of person.

We all can have a relationship with sex in its broadest sense: the stuff of life.

For all of you on the asexual spectrum that I may have alienated with my earlier writing or teachings, I apologize for my ignorance. I wish us all a more vast and inclusive relationship with the concept of sex than I used to have.

My definition of sex keeps expanding as I grow and learn, and I'm grateful for that. In the past, my definition was more narrow, because the definitions I got from my teachers and examples in my life were more narrow. And while the narrowest definitions can still be accurate, they do not include the sheer scope and scale of the unfolding cosmos and the power of nature.

As we are part of both the unfolding cosmos and the power of nature, our relationship with sex is as expansive as both of these.

WHAT IS SEX?

Sex is drive. Sex is connection. Sex is creativity. Sex can fuel rage or love. It's all about how we choose to channel the energy of life itself.

Sex is in a kiss. A breath. A touch. Sex arouses our genitals and ignites our imaginations. Sex is in a paintbrush on canvas, or a foot tracing patterns on the floor. Sex is in the dirt and all growing things. Sex is everywhere.

How we access the power of sex is our choice.

How we claim the power of sex is also our choice.

Coercion is violence. Consent is key.

Sex can involve genitals or it can not involve genitals. I've long balked at the word "foreplay" responding that "it is all sex." Foreplay means that only a certain act—usually the penetration of one person's body part with another person's body part—is considered to be sex.

As far as I'm concerned, the only good thing about the word foreplay is the play part.

Play is creative. Play harnesses life energy. Play is sex in its most expansive definition, and sex is also play. Exploration. Finding the pathways of life and pleasure.

Play expands our imagination.

Children play to learn. Children also play because they are so filled with life energy they must find multiple ways to channel and express it. They shriek for the sake of hearing their own voices. They run because running is fun. When a child interacts with the world, everything is new.

There are no boundaries until we are taught where the edges of ourselves exist.

There is no shame until we are trained into it.

Healthy and well cared for children have direct, innocent access to life energy. Wouldn't you like more of that?

Sex—access to life energy—shifts and changes with our life phases. At first, it is all innocent exploration of the wonder of life itself.

Next, sex is often pushed by internal hormonal shifts and changes as well as societal pressure and expectations: Have sex constantly! Don't have sex at all! If you enjoy the act of sex, you're a slut! If you don't want to engage in sexual activity, you're a freak!

We have all experienced some versions of these attitudes and either deflected or internalized them. Working with the sex point of the Iron Pentacle can help us reclaim our connection to pure life energy from all of these voices.

Some of us have abused or been abused in the name of sex. This is a twisted sense of the word. We can—often with help—

cleanse these old, damaging ways and work to heal (or make amends if we were the ones enacting harm).

What sort of activities and exploration can help us correct past wrongs, or heal ourselves, body, mind, and soul? How can grow into a healthier relationship with this energetic flow? The answers to these questions will be slightly different for each of us.

And, we can reclaim our own relationship to sex over time.

Then comes the rest of life….

QUESTIONS ABOUT LIFE AND SEX

What is our relationship to sex (or life energy) when we are ill?

What is our relationship to sex during aging?

What is our relationship to sex when we don't quite feel ourselves?

What is our relationship to sex when we feel fully ourselves?

What is our relationship to sex when we feel healthy and burgeoning with life?

It is useful to periodically visit these questions and spend some time living with them. Some questions will land more clearly in certain times of life, which is as it should be.

As I write this, I'm finally on the other side of seven years of a health crisis. Even through the worst of those times, I found ways to connect with life itself. Whether it was what I called "dragging my carcass around the block" during the most challenging parts of my illness, or struggling through physical therapy when a brain injury made even walking hard, I committed to showing up. I tested myself. I tried.

I'm not saying it was easy. I'm saying showing up felt necessary. Right now? I feel pretty good. I'm walking a lot outside or on my office walk pad, and am back to occasionally swinging kettlebells. I'm also in the creative flow a lot of time, which feels good.

None of that was possible a few years ago, though I kept creating through it all. My relationship with life force has shifted yet again. So have my romantic, love, and sex relationships and my friendships.

See what I mean about different questions for different times of life?

We will all die. But other than that, nothing is inevitable. Maintaining an active relationship with life force and sex can help us claim the best life we can possibly live.

SEX AND LIFE PHASES

I'd like to talk a bit more about our connection to life force, energy, and the flow of sex as our lives shift.

If you're a person who lives with clinical depression, for example, what are the best ways for you to connect to life when you feel ready to? Is it listening to music? Dancing? Talking with a friend? Getting outside under the trees?

And what helps you shift toward connection when that feels almost impossible? Can you go through some breathing exercises or stretches? Take your medication and notice the feel of water moving across your tongue and down your throat?

If you are a person going through hormonal changes, how can you find ways to access pleasure during this phase? What might that look or feel like for you? Does it look like finding clothing you feel comfortable and good in as your body changes? Does it feel like taking a bath or getting a massage? Does it look like prepping a colorful dinner for some friends? Singing karaoke? Plunging in the ocean? Finding a new way to masturbate?

I could come up with one hundred scenarios and questions, but the point is, we can all access life energy, sex, pleasure, and presence, even if it feels as if all we have is a trickle. What this takes is a commitment to noticing that life is happening, all around us, and inside us, whether we want it to or not.

Sometimes it's the opposite: because of biological or spiritual changes, our connection to life can sometimes feel more like a flood, and that can become overwhelming. We may want physical sex all the time—never getting enough—or to take up skydiving, or might find ourselves in a rush of creativity, barely able to keep up.

In those cases, how do we celebrate sex, but modulate it enough that laundry and our jobs and everything else gets attention, too? Meditation can help. Or spiritual exercises such as yoga or tai chi can help. Or we may want to intensify our exercise routine.

Why? We need proper channels for high levels of life energy and sex connection. We can learn to run that energy up and down in and around our bodies and energy fields, instead of constantly seeking someplace—or someone—outside ourselves at which to direct the flow.

PRACTICE:

Whether you feel high or low energy today, pause for a moment.

Imagine you can breathe energy up from the earth and through the soles of your feet. Now imagine that energy running up through your body, fountaining out the top of your head, falling back down, and starting the cycle all over again. Breathe in, rise up, exhale, and cascade back down.

As you get used to this process, imagine you can push the energy further up and further down. Adjust your posture if you can, to allow for an even, steady flow, until you feel both rooted and expansive, with energy flowing easily through your body and around your energy fields.

Once it feels like enough, return to a sense of center in your stomach or solar plexus area.

Give thanks.

EMOTIONS AND LIFE FORCE

What is your emotional connection to your current sex, energy, life force, and pleasure levels? How do you feel about the physical act we call sex? How do you feel about exercise? How do you feel about pleasure?

Our emotional states can offer us insight into our physical states, and vice versa. Just as the food we eat affects our energy levels and mood, so do our moods affect our energy levels and connection with our bodies.

This brings me to another topic, one which may feel comfortable for some of us, and nearly impossible to look at for others:

Worthiness.

Worthiness will come up again and again as we explore the Iron Pentacle. It crops up in Sex, Pride, Self, Power, and Passion.

Our sense of worth affects our ability to connect: to ourselves, to our work, to other humans, and to the world.

So today I ask us to breathe into our sense of self-worth as it connects to life flow, creativity, pleasure, and our bodies.

What helps boost your sense of self-worth in these realms? What diminishes it?

COURTING LIFE

What makes you feel juicy inside and out?

What sucks you dry?

How much time and energy are you spending on either of these? Your answer to that will tell you a lot about your current relationship to life force and sex.

If we consistently devote energy to things that drain us, our access to life diminishes. If we consistently devote energy to things that give us juice, our access to life increases.

We cannot always choose the conditions of our lives, but we can choose how we respond and what we wish to focus on. This is particularly true for those of us fortunate enough to lead lives of relative privilege: we have food, stable housing, and enough income to live on.

What happens when life feels like nothing but struggle? We can choose one small thing that brings us into greater touch with generative life force: Listen to a song. Take a walk. Eat a good meal. Share a laugh. Commune with a tree.

Sex can be liberatory. Sex can be a revelation. Can we think outside the bombardment of manufactured "sex" that surrounds us on billboards and ads, and in popular culture? "Sex sells" is an adage because humans long for connection to the stuff of life. But the sort of sex they're peddling is twisted, and designed to prey upon our insecurities and our lack.

In contrast, a healthy connection to life force fills us up. And feeling replete with life is a thing I wish for us all, even for one moment at a time.

PRACTICE:

Read this over as many times as you need to before starting, or do this phase by phase, reading each section before doing the practice.

If you are able, set your feet flat on the ground and stand or sit comfortably. If you are not able, find a position where your body is as open to energetic flow as it can be. Our intention is to sit, lie, or stand without crossed limbs or curling around ourselves.

As much as possible, arrange your limbs in an open posture.

Next, turn your attention to your genitals. For some of us, that might feel fraught, so be gentle here. Whatever your connection is to your current physical body, send a thought of thanks and blessing to those parts of yourself.

Then open your attention to the rest of your body and just breathe with yourself for a moment. Take your time. Imagine your breath filling your entire physical form. Just stay with the process of consciously breathing and connecting.

After you've done this for a while, imagine you can inhale through the area of your perineum or generative organs. As you inhale, squeeze your muscles, then hold for a few seconds. Exhale and release.

Each body is different, so you will find your own rhythm. Let go of trying to do this correctly. Do what your body and your emotions allow right now.

As you inhale, allow your spine to lengthen. As you exhale, allow your stomach muscles to contract. Again, listen to your body and adapt this as you need to.

As you inhale, allow your shoulders, head, and hips to adjust themselves naturally, without added tension.

Release your attempts to squeeze on the inhale, and just breathe as naturally as you can. Let your body feel as loose and relaxed as possible as you breathe.

If you're having trouble relaxing, tense as many muscles at once as possible on a big inhalation, and release on a big exhalation.

Then just be and breathe.

Notice how your body feels. Notice your emotional state. Notice your energy levels.

Then, say out loud, "I bless my body, as it is. I bless my connection to sex, to creative flow, and to life itself."

Blessed be.

RECLAIMING SEX

Sex gets blocked and twisted in many ways. What I call the overculture uses sex as a form of power-over, or to denigrate, some people, and build others up in unhealthy ways. Some of us get unhelpful or damaging messages from our families of origin, or religious upbringing, our friends or would-be lovers, or from movies, songs, and books.

The thing I'd like to emphasize here is that our relationship to sex is ours. It doesn't belong to anyone else, and it certainly should not be under the control of anyone else. Autonomy around our connection to life and sense of pleasure is key.

To become healthy adults, we must claim the sex point for ourselves. This is true whether or not we are a person who enjoys, wants, or engages in sex acts ourselves.

We can call back our connection to life force, to creativity, to pleasure, to sex.

We can claim the sex point for ourselves and our lives.

Shall we practice?

PRACTICE:

Read this through as many times as you need to before engaging with this exercise. If you find yourself filled with fear or tension just reading the words, start with the opening breathing exercise and work up to doing the rest. You are the one in charge here.

But regardless of our current relationship to the point of sex, I encourage us all to try. Some of us may just need more time.

Breathe in life force. Pause. Exhale connection with all living beings. Pause.

Breathe in life force. Pause. Exhale connection with all living beings. Pause.

Breathe in life force. Pause. Exhale connection with all living beings. Pause...

Think of your relationship to your body, to creativity, to life, and to what we call sex. Think of all the places you may have given away your autonomy in this realm.

Where have you left your sex energy? Where and when has it been stolen from you? Where and when has it been squashed or suppressed?

On each inhalation, begin the process of calling sex back.

Call sex back from everyone who tried to make you feel uncomfortable in your body.

Call sex back from whomever assigned you a sex or gender at birth.

Call sex back from any person or institution who told you to be quiet and still. To not express your creativity.

Call sex back from every lover you've ever had. Call sex back from every lover you've longed for who did not reciprocate.

Call sex back from moments of coercion or nonconsensual dominance.

Call sex back from violence.

Call sex back from disapproval.

Call sex back from fear.

Call sex back from any person, institution, or situation that diminished your connection to life force.

Call sex back.

Breathe it in.

Expand around it.

Say, "I claim life. I claim creativity. I claim my relationship to sex."

Fill up with life. Fill up with the energy of sex, whatever that looks or feels like to you.

PART II: THE IRON AND PEARL PENTACLES

Keep breathing.

Keep claiming your right to the energy and flow of sex.

PRIDE

When drawing an invoking pentagram on our bodies, the energy flows from the head to our right foot. We name this point Pride.

To live with pride in a world that often wants to diminish us, or conversely, to have us lord it over others, is to commit to upending the systems of oppression.

Don't believe me? Think of how different your life might be if others celebrated your accomplishments. If they cherished your presence. If they were not trying to manipulate or squeeze you into a form that is more useful to them, or more to their liking.

Some of you may have been raised with people who supported you in these ways. I want to take a moment and celebrate *that*. What a wonderful circumstance!

Others of us—especially the neurodivergent, or the unruly, or the disabled, or the non-white, or non-cisgender, or poor, or queer, or...—haven't always had this experience. We were trained either to make ourselves smaller or puff ourselves up.

To unlearn these harmful patterns is to invoke healing and a sense of inner stability.

We can move toward a healthy sense of pride that is not contingent upon anyone else's opinion. And we can encourage our friends, comrades, and loved ones to do the same.

WHAT IS PRIDE?

Pride is knowing and claiming our place in the world. When we move in pride, we move with the assurance that we have a part to play in the cosmos, and that our part is important.

Not more important than anyone else's part, but important nonetheless.

If we think of the cosmos as a body, we are each a cell inside that body. Each cell in our own bodies has a boundary, a center, and a purpose that it enacts in concert with all the cells around it. That's us.

Pride is neither arrogance nor self-deprecation. Pride rides the shifting balance of our lives, adapting itself to our sense of power, place, and purpose.

In this way, pride is a cousin to true humility. To be truly humble is to have an ongoing awareness of how we fit into the world.

Many of us need to wrestle with inner voices or outer messages in order to come into right relationship with pride. If we were raised with messages telling us that pride is arrogance, or that pride will be our downfall, we might have a real struggle. The same is true for those of us raised by people or institutions who used shaming as a weapon. And as we hopefully know, shame is not a good vehicle for positive change, let alone self-growth.

And for others of us, taking up space put us in the line of fire, so we decided that our place in the world needed to be as small and hidden as possible. We adapted ourselves to what felt like a hostile world in the only way we knew how.

And some of us? We were taught that the only way to be successful in the world was to take up more space than anyone else, to be louder and act more entitled. We pushed against, or sometimes trampled, boundaries and masked pain with a lack of caring.

Take a breath now, and ask yourself if any of the above scenarios feel familiar. And if they don't, what were your formative experiences around the concept of pride? What shaped your sense of presence in the world?

This all links to our sense of self, of course, which is the next stop in our journey. What we are doing here is finding the connections between what others imposed upon or nurtured within us, and who we have become.

Examining our old stories helps us figure out the roots of our relationship to pride. Awareness of past influences increases our ability to heal and become whole.

A person raised to leverage arrogance as a form of power over others will have a different trajectory toward health and balance than a person who was constantly shamed and belittled. And of course, for any of these tactics used to control us, there can be any number of combinations of the above.

Sometimes an arrogant person is using this as a defense because an out-of-balance person used their own arrogance to enact cycles of shame. So, to break out of the shame cycle, the person internalized that they needed to lord it over others themselves.

An insecure person might have a brain wired toward anxiety and need to find support or medication to work through that and come into a sense of pride. A person who was shamed or harmed for simply existing might have trouble finding ways to contribute to the world. They have trouble taking their place, because doing so felt too dangerous. They hide their light and diminish what they can offer to the rest of us.

I could detail a thousand examples like this, but hopefully, in examining your own life, you will come to understand what influences have shaped you. Dig a bit deeper, and you might even uncover how and why.

PRACTICE:
What enters your mind when you think of pride? What does it feel like in your body? Does thinking about pride make you feel loose and expansive, or uneasy and diminished?

Who or what has caused you to feel diminished or ashamed? What would you like to reclaim regarding pride?

ABDICATING PRIDE

To avoid pride is to avoid responsibility. This might seem like a strange thing for me to say, but I believe that it is true. More than belief, I have experienced this as true.

I'll give an example. Years ago, when I was teaching a lot, I was sometimes working with others who refused to claim the title of teacher. "I'm just a facilitator," they would say, sometimes seeming a bit smug about it. "Not a teacher."

This made me shake my head for three reasons. First of all, good facilitation is a hard, and requires training and a very specific skillset. Not just anyone can just plop down and facilitate a group of people. So, they were disrespecting facilitators.

Second, by not claiming the role of teacher, I felt they were abdicating responsibility to the people they were teaching. Sure, the folks showing up to learn were all adults and could take care of themselves, but that did not mean those of us taking on teaching roles did not hold some measure of responsibility to treat them and the material with respect, and to foster a proper learning environment.

Third, teaching is its own skillset. By claiming to not be a teacher, yet taking on a teaching role, these people were disrespectful to teaching itself, as well as disrespectful to the students. Without even realizing it, they were saying that teaching took no skill or preparation and that they had done neither.

None of this was true, of course. At least I hope not. By not claiming to be teachers in that moment, these people were diminishing both themselves and the process we were all a part of. They had no sense of pride.

Pride can lead us more deeply into respect for ourselves and others. Conversely, both arrogance and self-deprecation can be weaponized against others, and an abdication of taking on what is rightfully ours to uphold.

. . .

PRACTICE:

When have you allowed arrogance or self-diminishment abdicate responsibility for something you could have taken on? Why do you think you allowed this to happen, or even caused this to happen?

What was or can be a correction to this lack of pride?

EMOTIONS AND PRIDE

What is your emotional connection to your current sense of pride? When thinking about pride, do you feel squeamish? Ashamed? Confident? Overbearing? Comfortable?

How do you feel about your work, your creativity, your accomplishments? How do you feel about your perceived failures? Do you tie your sense of pride to others' responses? Do you transfer your sense of pride to the accomplishments of others?

How does your relationship to pride affect your physical body and vice versa? How do your emotional states affect your relationship to pride and vice versa?

What insight can you gain from these realizations?

And here we are at worthiness, which I said would appear in many of these points.

Do you feel worthy because of what you have done or learned, or perhaps undone and unlearned?

Do you feel worthy to simply be in this world?

Knowing that we have worth as we are, no matter what we produce or accomplish, is a strong move toward claiming a healthy sense of pride.

OPENING TO PRIDE

Right now, what is one thing you feel proud of?

Are you doing well at taking care of yourself, your communities, or your family? Have you gotten some creative time in? Did you meditate or exercise? Finish a project? Take time to reflect and be quiet? Get some extra sleep? Make a hard decision? Push yourself out of your usual zone?

What is your relationship with pride? Do you struggle with the concept? Were you taught that pride was a bad thing, akin to arrogance?

Healthy pride helps us return to a balanced sense of self.

We can know our worth. The more we claim our worth, the harder it is for us to be manipulated by forces outside of ourselves, or the mean voices in our heads. The less easily manipulated we are, the more autonomy we retain. The more autonomy we have, the better able we are to help the world around us.

When we acknowledge and claim our place in the world, we recognize the part we play in the interdependent dance of the cosmos.

This feels especially important in a world where billionaires and multinational corporations hold the bulk of power over others. We are bombarded daily with messages telling us we are not enough, and should buy this thing that will mask that. We are inundated with messages telling us we have no power and might as well give up.

While living within these conditions, cultivating pride helps to shift the balance of power. The more people who live in true pride, the more easily we can join together to build something better. If I know my worth, and you know yours, we can tap into our skills and talents and help each other. This ripples out, touching everything around us. And that is how positive change is wrought.

Do you know your worth? And again: What are you most feeling proud of today?

What would your life be like if you claimed your worth?

This is not about self-aggrandizement. Nor is it about self-deprecation. Both of these are things we'll discuss more later. Both of these are shadows of pride, and not pride itself.

Pride is not arrogance. To have pride is to have clarity about ourselves and our accomplishments.

If pride is about knowing our place in the world, what helps us do that?

PRACTICE:

Let's begin with a quick assessment. Set aside fifteen minutes with pen and paper, and write the answers to these questions. If writing feels hard right now, allow yourself to go for a walk or take a bath while pondering these questions first:

What is one of my talents?
What do I find interesting?
How do I show up to help?

SUPERPOWERS

One facet of true pride and true humility that often gets overlooked is what we might call our personal superpower. Why is this overlooked? Because usually our personal superpower is something that is so natural to us, so innate, that we don't even notice it.

But rest assured, other people feel its effects.

This superpower might be the ability to easily organize a group of volunteers. It might be the ability to break a stalemate. To shift a conversation. To make the connections that allow others to share resources or help one another or themselves. It might mean having a vision in the midst of chaos and being able to communicate that vision. It might be an ability to deeply listen. It might be speaking the blunt truth. It might be noticing patterns and articulating them in useful ways.

The more we work with pride, the better able we are to start noticing the affect we have on the world around us. The clearer we become about this, the more we notice our superpower.

And this, for me, is the place where pride and humility truly intersect. My superpower of making connections just is. For me, it is nothing special, it's just something that my brain and personality tend to do.

Now that I know this, I can move in the world from this awareness and leverage that superpower, that strength. I acknowledge my ability and the ways in which it has helped others in the past, usually in small and subtle ways.

Becoming aware of my superpower has increased my ability to know and claim a place in my communities. If I see something that might be of use to a friend or colleague, I'll pass it along. If I'm in conversation with a person working on a project to bring Black science fiction and fantasy book vending machines to crowded coffee shops, and I know that another person in the room works for a café, I'll make the introduction.

If a friend is getting an air conditioner upgrade, I'll pass their old one along to another friend helping elders during a heat wave.

All of this comes as naturally to me as your personal superpower does to you. That is, if you allow yourself to express it.

Again, you may notice the ways in which this conversation already begins to lead us into the point of Self. A sense of pride increases our sense of self. All the points of the pentacles flow with one another, which can make it tricky to figure out which one we are speaking of exactly.

Is my superpower a part of self? Of course it is. But recognizing that superpower is a form of pride. Once I recognize my abilities and gifts, I carry those into my sense of self. In finding pride (and humility) in this facet of myself, I can leverage it in my communities.

Before I recognized this, I sometimes felt I was being pushy or intrusive, inserting myself into people's business. After recognizing this, I found ways to foster these connections that come from a sense of place, and a sense of pride. This has made me more effective. Allowing my ordinary superpower to flourish helps my small corner of the world.

Practice:

What do you think your superpower is? How does it express itself in your life? What is your relationship with this superpower? Do you respect it? Accept it? Feel a sense of pride in it? Or does it make you feel uncomfortable or wary? Or can you not even notice it at all? Take a breath. If you can't notice your superpower, you might screw up the courage to ask a friend or colleague what they think you bring to relationships or community. If you struggle with honoring your superpower, can you make a short list of the ways it might be of help and service to others? And if you feel a sense of pride, how can you celebrate that?

RECLAIMING PRIDE

Pride gets blocked, suppressed, or puffed up.

The overculture—especially as influenced by some religions—uses pride as bludgeon to keep us in line. It particularly doesn't want those of us deemed as unworthy to have a healthy sense of our place in the world. Instead, we are "put in our place" in a position of being less-than, rather than equals. Others are gifted large swathes of privilege and power-over, and they are said to be rightfully proud, though that is more often arrogance masquerading as pride, and not pride at all.

"Don't get too big for your britches," an old saying goes. Or, even older still, "don't get airs above your station."

These messages are designed to make us smaller than we are, and to enforce distinctions of class, wealth, and other privileged positions.

But, as with sex energy, our relationship to pride is our own. Our worth is not contingent upon anyone else's opinion, or our race, gender, sexuality, economic status, physical or mental abilities, or any other socially constructed markers.

To live as we wish, we would do well to recognize that we play a vital role in the unfolding of the story of the world. It may feel small, but think of the impact the smallest cell in our bodies has on the whole. Without that cell, everything would function differently.

The cell doesn't have to know or claim its place, it simply is.

We can work toward the same.

We can call back our sense of place. We can claim our abilities, skills, talents, and worth.

We can claim the pride point for ourselves and our lives.

Shall we practice?

Practice:

Read this through as many times as you need to before engaging with this exercise. Remember, you are the one in charge here.

Breathe in life force. Pause. Exhale connection with all living beings. Pause.

Breathe in life force. Pause. Exhale connection with all living beings. Pause.

Breathe in life force. Pause. Exhale connection with all living beings. Pause...

Think of your relationship to your place: in work, your spiritual communities, your family, society, and the cosmos. Think of all the places you may have given away your pride to those people or institutions who may wish to control you, or whom you fear, whether for good reasons or bad.

Where have you left your sense of pride? Where and when has it been stolen from you? Undermined? Where and when has it been squashed or suppressed?

On each inhalation, begin the process of calling pride back.

Call pride back from everyone who tried to bully or belittle you.

Call pride back from any person or institution who told you

to know your place, as long as that place was being small, quiet, or subservient.

Call pride back from every person who puffed you up as a form of manipulation.

Call pride back from every person or institution who tried to fill you with shame.

Call pride back from arrogance.

Call pride back from uncertainty.

Call pride back from fear.

Call pride back from any person, institution, or situation that diminished your ability to take up space in the world.

Call pride back.

Breathe it in.

Expand around it.

Say, "I claim my place. I claim my abilities. I claim my worth. I claim pride."

Fill up with breath. Fill up with the energy of pride, whatever that looks or feels like to you.

Keep breathing.

Keep claiming your right to the energy and flow of pride.

SELF

When drawing an invoking pentagram on our bodies, the energy flows from our right foot to our left hand. We name this point Self.

"Know Thyself," the Oracle of Delphi tells us. But what does that mean? How do we come to know the self?

Do we gain our sense of self from the reflections and responses of others? Is it a feeling that arises inside us?

Are we our work, our hobbies, or our gender, our income, our race, or some other social markers?

To claim ourselves is to claim both our core essence and as many of our facets as we can. This includes the parts of self that are hidden from our consciousness, and plumbed through therapy, magic, or dreams.

Are you who others think you are? Or are you something else? Do you shrink your weirdness or use it as a shield? Are you comfortable in your own skin, or uneasy?

All of these are questions that help us uncover the nature of our self and the relationship we have with our inner being.

We can examine any patterns we might have where we shape ourselves according to the wishes of others and learn to become more wholly who we are and who we wish to be.

To live with self is to seek our truth.

What might it be like to live in a world where others do the same?

And how do we allow each other room to be, to breathe, to make decisions, to grow, to fall, to change?

PRACTICE:

What enters your mind when you think of self? What does it feel like in your body? Does thinking about self make you feel comfortable? Happy? Uneasy?

Who or what has caused you to feel as if you were not enough? What would you like to reclaim regarding self?

WHAT IS SELF?

Self is not all the masks and personalities we show the world, though those masks and personalities are part of what we call self.

Self is, at root, our core essence. Self is the song, or light, or sensation that is left shimmering inside us when all our outer trappings are stripped away.

Does the idea of that frighten you? Interest you? Take a breath into that feeling, either way.

Self is something we grow into. There are glimmers of self in the youngest infant and the smallest child. But the world begins to shape us from the moment we take breath. We are treated in different ways by different people. We are loved or barely tolerated. We are assigned qualities according to our perceived gender, our family's social class, or other circumstances.

All of this builds what we think of as self but can also bury who we truly are inside.

To uncover self requires curiosity and diligence.

Self is neither aggrandizement or deprecation. Both of those are, instead, shields and protections we put up to hide ourselves from the world. These are learned behaviors in a world that has taught us it isn't safe, or that we must make ourselves more acceptable to others.

This is often a survival technique, and one that some of us use consistently, and others, situationally.

So who are we without these coping mechanisms? Have these propped-up shells become our sense of self? Can we reclaim who we truly are, or who we are becoming?

We can. It takes some courage, but it is possible.

PRACTICE:

Let's begin by asking some questions. Feel free to read each question, then close your eyes and ponder. Or perhaps you'd like to journal your answers. Either or both techniques will be useful.

How much alone time do you need? How much do you allow yourself?

How much time with others do you need? How much do you allow yourself?

These questions also help us to uncover more of our essential nature.

Next:

Take a breath, and drop into your center. Breathe again. What is there? What is at your core? And what does this core part of you desire? Does it want to be known? Does it want to create, or be of service, or simply be?

There are no wrong answers here, only exploration.

For the self to be free, it needs room to be.

What is stopping you from understanding self?

What encourages you to deepen your relationship to self?

Breathe into your core. You are who you are, right now.

And that is good.

UNDERMINING AND STRENGTHENING SELF

In examining our relationship to self, it is helpful to notice the ways in which we undermine ourselves. This links back to pride, of course. If we were raised to cultivate shame or arrogance, we may have grown into deprecation or aggrandizement of self.

Neither self-deprecation nor aggrandizement are healthy or balanced ways of being in the world. Both of these states, curiously, come from a form of self-centeredness and insecurity.

Think about it. Extreme insecurity makes a person feel as if they are the center of the universe for everyone: People are laughing at me. People are talking about me. People dislike me.

In reality, other than bullies, most people are too busy thinking of their own lives to focus that much on us.

A different form of insecurity is feeling completely unnoticed, or wishing to disappear.

And a third form of insecurity is self-aggrandizement. We must push ourselves forward as better than others because to be similar or equal to others threatens our sense of self.

All three of these states are signs of an insecure ego born of the conditions of our upbringing, the wiring of our brains, or our fight for survival. And don't think I'm using the phrase "insecure ego" as an insult. I am not.

None of these states are wrong responses. Wishing to protect the self is a natural reaction to a variety of factors.

That said, over time, these states aren't the most helpful ways of being in the world, and tend to force us into boxes or bubbles we might not wish to live in long term, even if they feel temporarily safe.

So, how to counteract any of these?

That will look and feel different for each of us. For some of us, therapy is the answer. Or medication. Or learning to notice our patterns and practicing interrupting these patterns over time. Journaling might give us insight. Asking a close friend to help us notice our patterns can also be useful.

Whatever the answer is for you, only you can say. It is yourself, after all.

Practice:

Take out a journal, or some paper, or your favorite writing application. Set a timer for ten minutes.

Write down any patterns of self-deprecation, self-erasure, or self-aggrandizement you notice in yourself (and even others). What do you notice about these patterns? What might they have to teach you?

Really stretch yourself with this. For example, if you tend toward self-erasure, are there forms of aggrandizement you may not be noticing? Defense mechanisms can be sneaky!

If you need to do a second ten-minute session to dig a bit deeper, go ahead.

Next, for the following month, try to notice these patterns or tendencies as they arise. Do they happen in all situations, or only under certain conditions? And how do these tendencies make you feel?

In what way are they serving the life you have, and how are they undermining the life you wish to lead?

EMOTIONS AND SELF

What is your emotional response when you think of, or tune into, yourself?

Do you hold yourself tenderly?

Do you speak words of censure or love to yourself?

Do you cringe when thinking of yourself?

Do you feel pride in yourself?

What makes you feel angry about yourself? Or sad? Or joyous?

If your emotional responses to self are consistently undermining or on the so-called negative end of the spectrum, do you want to change that?

What are some ways you might go about doing so?

If your sense of self feels balanced and strong, how can you celebrate or appreciate that in your life?

PRACTICE:

Each morning, practice letting your first thought on awaking be: "I love you."

Say that—internally or out loud—to yourself and then to the world.

For many of us, this will be a very difficult practice. That is okay. Please keep trying.

SELF AND COMMUNITY

Without a stable sense of self, it can be very difficult to form healthy, nurturing relationships. We become prone to reaction to others, and shape ourselves accordingly, rather than showing up as we are. This might even take the form of preemptive behavioral changes, trying to stave off challenging situations in advance.

Or we may try to control others as a way of making ourselves feel safer or more in power.

What happens when a whole group of people who don't have a steady or well-integrated sense of self try to work together?

There is jockeying for position.

There is people pleasing.

There are conflicts over power structures.

There are a lot of unwritten rules we either try to uphold or smash.

Clear communication becomes suspect or difficult.

Bad faith can be assumed.

I'm sure we can all add to this list of issues that arise, because we've all experienced variations on work, family, or community drama.

Make no mistake: I'm not saying that all conflict is bad. Conflict can be a healthy and necessary way to work out differences or come to deeper accord, or even to find that there needs to be a parting of ways.

Some of us—me included—have had to learn how to be in healthy conflict and know that the world won't fall apart if we allow ourselves to get angry, sad, or to disagree.

But some conflict is unnecessary and causes extra stress on our relationships.

There are too often subterranean issues masquerading as surface disagreements. But being more honest with each other requires becoming more honest with ourselves.

Again: I'm not talking about "brutal" honesty or even radical honesty. There is a deeper form of honesty, a truth that arises from something we'll spend time on later: compassion.

When our hearts are open to ourselves and the selves of others, we can meet one another with greater grace, even in conflict, assuming good faith instead of bad, and invoking a willingness to work together, to build and grow.

We can bring this effort into all areas of our lives, including our parasocial relationships with people online, or with distant friends, coworkers, and acquaintances.

Making an effort to be more present in all our relationships can also make it easier to walk away when a friendship, workplace, or situation simply doesn't work for us anymore.

Often, the healthier our sense of self becomes, the more our relationships winnow themselves down because we're no longer willing to shove ourselves into certain shapes in order to belong.

Other relationships may arrive or expand because we've made space for them. Or we may discover contentment in our own company, and find pleasure in solitude.

Practice:

What is your current sense of self? How does that impact your relationships with close friends, at work, or in your communities?

How honest are you with yourself and others?

How do you feel in your relationships: at home, at work, in practice, or at play?

Is there space for your deeper self to be present in the world?

Can you invite others to share themselves more honestly, as well?

EXPLORING THE SELF TO COME

What would your best self look or feel like?

When we're caught up in the day-to-day of paying for housing and food, taking care of family members, drinking enough water, dealing with our mental and physical health, making sure the chores get done...it can be hard to make enough space to even assess what we want our lives to look like and who we want to be while living that life.

So today, I'd like to invite us all to daydream a little. When you imagine your ideal life, who is the person living it? What strengths and weaknesses does that person have? What passions, talents, and skills? What do they most enjoy? What does their day consist of? What sort of work do they do? What are their relationships like? Do they engage in service to community? What does their home feel like?

Really let yourself explore, allowing your imagination to play.

How far from your current life does this daydream feel? What changes in your self might you want to explore in order to manifest such a dream?

There's a spell I've done a few times in my life when I wanted or needed to shift the way my life was running. I'll offer it below. You can do this practice two ways, and may wish to do first one, and then the other.

PRACTICE:

One, daydream about how you'd like to inhabit the world. What sort of self would you like to be? Working from your core out, start adding or subtracting qualities or practices you'd like to incorporate into your personal sense of self. Don't worry about what other people might perceive. This is about you.

Now, what sort of spiritual practice, physical practice, mental health practice, etc., might help support this self?

Two: What sort of life would you like to inhabit in one year's time? What is your home like? Does work feel satisfying? Do you have enough resources to share? What sort of relationships would you like?

Don't pinpoint down too many specifics. We need to allow room for the universe to meet us. Instead, say, "I'd like to live in a warm, comfortable space with room for my cats and friends. I want to manifest work that pays well, where I can use my skills and talents, working around people who appreciate me...." You get the picture.

Now, for the rest of the spell. Once you have daydreamed and then written down what you wish for self and/or life in general, check to see if it feels right to change the language at all. Maybe "I'd like to" or "I want" needs to change to "I will." Test out the words and notice what resonates.

Next, write or type it out. Then let it rest for a few days, or even a month. Let the spell percolate. Then look at it again. Does it still feel right? Make what adjustments you need to.

When the spell finally feels set, write or type it out in red—if you've done this on a computer, print it out when you're done. Charge up the spell. You can do this in different ways; for example, fold the paper and burn a candle over it for a week or a month. Every time you light the candle, say something like, "I will manifest the life that supports my healthiest and best self," or words that feel right to you. Spend a few moments, centered and breathing, holding the feeling or image of this self or life in your mind.

Then put the paper away somewhere safe. Check on it again in six months.

What did you end up manifesting for yourself in that time? What has changed?

CALLING BACK SELF

As I wrote earlier, our sense of self is shaped by many things.

How often have you given your self away?

How often have you hidden who you truly are?

How often have you adjusted yourself to please or placate others?

How often have you masked who you are in order to stay safe or to get ahead or to win some perceived status game?

The good thing is, like with all the points on the Iron Pentacle, we can call back and reclaim Self. This practice will be similar for all the points, but I encourage us to go through them, point by point, until we feel a greater sense of wholeness.

PRACTICE:

Read this through as many times as you need to before engaging with this exercise. Remember, you are the one in charge here.

Breathe in life force. Pause. Exhale connection with all living beings. Pause.

Breathe in life force. Pause. Exhale connection with all living beings. Pause.

Breathe in life force. Pause. Exhale connection with all living beings. Pause...

Think of your relationship to your place: in work, your spiritual communities, your family, society, and the cosmos. Think of all the places you may have given away your sense of self to those people or institutions who may wish to control you, or whom you fear, whether for good reasons or bad.

Where have you left your sense of self? Where and when has it been stolen from you? Undermined? Where and when has it been squashed or suppressed?

On each inhalation, begin the process of calling self back.

Call self back from everyone who tried to tell you who you ought to be.

Call self back from any person or institution who told you how to think, feel, act, and how to be.

Call self back from every person who love-bombed you or belittled you as forms of manipulation.

Call self back from every person or institution who tried to squeeze you into a box of their own making.

Call self back from deprecation.

Call self back from aggrandizement.

Call self back from fear.

Call self back from any person, institution, or situation that diminished your ability to shine, as you truly are.

Call self back.

Breathe it in.

Expand around it.

Say, "I claim my own being. I claim my values. I claim my core. I claim self."

Fill up with breath. Fill up with the energy of self, whatever that looks or feels like to you.

Keep breathing.

Keep claiming your right to the energy and flow of self.

POWER

When drawing an invoking pentagram on our bodies, the energy flows from our left hand, across our hearts, and into our right hand. We name this point Power.

When you think of the word power, what is your first response? Are you repelled? Intrigued? Wistful? Anxious? Engaged?

That gut response tells us a lot about our relationship to power in our own lives and in the world.

When you think of the word power, who comes to mind? Yourself? A loved one? A teacher? A politician? A businessperson?

That image also tells us a lot about our relationship to power. So many of us seek power or avoid power. We fear power or loathe power.

This is because what I call the overculture has given us a skewed idea of what power actually is and how it acts in the world. The most prevalent examples of power in the world are most often those people who are using what writer Starhawk called "power-over."

There are still more kinds of power. There is the power innate in each of us. There is also collective power, which is one of the strongest powers we have access to as human beings. Collective power takes effort and time, of course, and it helps if we are each tapped into our personal power. But collective power is possible and quite effective.

There are other kinds of power as well. The power of the ocean. The power of wind and fire. The power of glaciers, carving canyons. The power of time. The power of an osprey diving for a fish. The power of stars giving birth to more stars.

The power of love.

PRACTICE:

What enters your mind when you think of power? What does it feel like in your body? Does thinking about power make you feel comfortable? Happy? Uneasy?

What is your current relationship to power in your life? What would you like to reclaim?

WHAT IS POWER?

Power is our ability to do.

Power is connected to Self because it stems from an inner sense of our abilities. The stronger our sense of self and our own worth becomes, the stronger our relationship with power grows.

Power is also our ability to choose. The more we feel our choices are curtailed, the less power we experience inside.

I'm not talking about the sort of choices that pester and beleaguer our days and our minds: What soap to buy? What cause to support? What school? What brand of gum? What social media platform? Who to listen to? Whom to believe?

I'm speaking of the deeper choices: What sorts of lives do we wish to live? What sort of people do we want to become? What sort of society do we want to help build?

Sometimes this means throwing away the too-many-options-to-choose entirely. To walk away from the choices of distraction and to, instead, choose meaning.

That is all on an individual level but it also applies to our collective power. The more we reach out to each other, the better able we are to get things done. To rest when we need to. To show up with all of our abilities, talents, and skills. To show up with our hopes and our fears.

When my power meets your power, there is so much we can build.

Those who wield large amounts of power-over-others fear both our individual power and, even more, our collective power. They love to keep us distracted by too many petty choices, by fighting with each other for scraps, or scrambling to get our basic needs met.

What will it take for us to pause, breathe, and begin to cultivate inner and collective power?

That answer will be slightly different for each of us, but one thing I know:

We can do this.

. . .

PRACTICE:

Journal or meditate on the following questions. Really take your time with them. Ask your loved ones and your friends.

How much personal power and autonomy do you feel? How much do you allow yourself?

How much collective power do you see in your communities? How can you foster this?

GIVING AWAY OUR POWER

There are very real systems of oppression and limitation that we live within and among. It becomes easy to see our power being stolen by unscrupulousness, cruelty, and greed. But in order to confront these systems, we need to claim our internal power.

We can practice claiming the fire in belly, heart, and mind—which we will explore more in the section on passion.

We can call our power back from every person who tried to keep us from claiming our abilities, or who tried to tell us that we could not *do*.

But first, we must begin to notice the ways in which we have given our power away in the past, and may still be giving over our power to others. Sometimes, this is a simple—and difficult—as noticing where we have sloppy boundaries and slowly practicing shoring them up.

Poor boundaries are not a failure; they are simply a habit, often borne of childhood experiences or a series of events that told us it was safer to do what we thought was expected of us, rather than what it felt most powerful or correct to do.

In other cases, poor boundaries may give us a false sense of power, including power over others and a sense of place in the world. Who always has the most cutting gossip? Is that you, or some of the people you surround yourself with? Are you always up in other people's business while ignoring your own? What sort of reward do you get from shoring up someone else's patterns or behavior rather than increasing your power by minding your own work?

Let me be clear: I am not talking here of gossip as an important vehicle to share news or information. I am not talking about helping friends with their troubles. I am talking about feeding energy to patterns that end up leaving us in continuous states of imbalance, with no real sense of power to call our own.

If we are always seeking power or approval from people or situations outside of ourselves, this is no different from giving our power away.

Power is seated within us, in our most centered selves.

If power is the ability to do, then how do we want to spend our time? What exactly will we choose?

So, how do we practice reclaiming our own power? We begin by noticing our behavior, emotions, and patterns. Then we take responsibility for our actions, our attitudes, and our conditions, as much as is feasible.

We may not be able to move away from the toxic waste center that gives us headaches, but perhaps we can call back some power by gathering our neighbors to help publicize the bad environmental practices happening in the area. That is one form of calling back our power.

We may have a physical or mental disability that makes certain aspects of our lives challenging. But maybe we can call back some power by establishing boundaries around when and how we work. Also, demanding accommodation around small workplace changes is a form of calling back our power.

There are myriad forms of calling back our power. We all need to find the ways that work for us.

That's a form of claiming power, too.

PRACTICE:

What is one area of life you want to call your power back from? There might be several, but this week, start with just one. Then choose one thing this week that will push the edges of your comfort zone and expand your sense of power.

Do that thing.

EMOTIONS AND POWER

What is your emotional response when you think of, or tune into, your own power?

Do you cave in?

Do you sit taller?

Do you tell yourself that power is a bad, corrupting force that you want nothing to do with?

Do you ask, "Who am I to carry myself with a sense of power?"

Do you feel your inner strength and honor that?

What makes you feel excited by cultivating personal power?

Are you galvanized by calling your power back?

Do you fear punishment if you call your power back?

What other emotions come up when you sense or think of your personal power?

What might you like to change about those responses?

What might you wish to strengthen?

How would you do that? What is one step?

We can celebrate the power we have and the power we are growing into. We can celebrate the small things and the large.

It is often the subtlest internal shifts that manifest the greatest effects. We can carry our power with both lightness and responsibility. In doing so, we can better share our power with community and friends.

Practice:

Every day, find a posture that allows breath and energy to flow freely and strongly through your body. For most of us, that means allowing our spines to rise up from our pelvis, letting our shoulders roll back and drop, and placing our head in alignment with our spine.

Once you have found a posture that feels balanced, allow yourself to breathe.

This may take a lot of practice. Some of our bodies may need assistance in cultivating a posture that allows for this clear energetic flow.

For some of us, though? A few minor adjustments to our posture are all we need.

POWER IN COMMUNITY

Imagine yourself with a strong sense of your own power, abilities, gifts, and talents.

Now, imagine yourself in community. Imagine yourself in

family, at work, in your temple or coven, volunteering, engaging in mutual aid, or any number of scenarios where working in concert with others is the key to success.

Imagine yourself, in your own power, being willing to share power with others in the group. How do they respond? Are they welcoming? Do they seem excited? Are they fearful, jealous, or jockeying for position?

When a group is healthy, people are willing to show up and share power. They are willing to say, "This is outside my ability or skill set. Are you willing to teach me about it, or are you able to take this part on while I do this other task?"

When conflict arises in a healthy group, if there are systems or protocols in place to address that conflict, each member is supported to remain in their own power while lending strength to the group, and vice versa. The group lends strength to the process.

When conflict arises in a not-so-healthy group, one person or people might feel squashed down, diminished, or unheard, while others take over. There is jockeying for positions of prestige. Some people do most of the work while others end up as hangers-on.

I want to talk a bit about the "some people do most of the work" dynamic. In some cases, the people doing most of the work are doing so because they can't bear to share power or responsibility. This sets up a terrible dynamic that serves no one and causes burnout or fracturing of the group.

In other cases, the people doing most of the work are taking on all of the unwanted, unglamorous tasks that those in positions of leadership don't want, while those in leadership make all the decisions.

Neither scenario is sustainable or a sign that a group is willing to practice power sharing.

I'm not saying that groups don't need leadership or organizing or coordination. I'm just saying there are far more equitable ways to go about this than some structures might imply.

To shift the overculture toward equity, justice, and shared power, we must begin to examine our closer-in communities and how they operate. Are the people best suited for certain tasks given rein to complete them in the way that feels best to them? Or are they micromanaged by others? Does everyone have some say in the overall structure of the group? Do people with the most longevity and buy-in have more weight?

All of this shifts from group to group. I've seen groups where new members have to fight to be heard at all, and in contrast, seen other groups where a brand-new person was allowed to come in and derail something others had worked hard on for months, in the name of giving them an equal voice.

Power shifts according to how much every group members' abilities and actions are honored and recognized.

There is no one way to share power. We get to figure it out, together, deferring to each other's skills and expertise, while still honoring what each person brings to the table.

As it has been often said: power shared is power multiplied.

Together, we are more powerful than we are alone.

PRACTICE ONE:
What do you notice about power dynamics in your family, friend group, workplace, or various communities?

What part are you most comfortable playing?

What might help you and your communities to share power more gracefully?

PRACTICE TWO:

What is your vision for your own power? How would you like it to feel inside? How might it manifest?

What is your vision for community power?

Picture a community, a family, a workplace, a country, a coven, a temple, a grove where power is shared, problems are addressed, and people's skills, talents, and natures are nurtured and supported.

Breathe that in.

Write it down. Dance it. Draw it. Sing it.

Believe that it can be.

CALLING BACK POWER

By examining power, and our relationship to it, we have already begun the process of calling it back.

How often have you given your power away, or had your sense of power taken from you?

Did it start in childhood? At school? Among friends? With bullies?

How about at work? On the street? Within the halls of government?

Do you feel as if your power has been stolen from you?

Have you given away your power in order to keep the peace?

Have you given away your power in order to stay safe?

Have you given away your power by refusing to take responsibility for your actions or reactions?

Have you given away your power by not holding others accountable for their actions or reactions?

There are myriad ways we may have given our powers to others or—as in the case of severe status imbalances—feel as if our power has been taken away.

No matter what the situation, or how many times it has happened…

We can call our power back.

PRACTICE:

Read this through as many times as you need to before engaging with this exercise. Remember, you are the one in charge here.

Breathe in life force. Pause. Exhale connection with all living beings. Pause.

Breathe in life force. Pause. Exhale connection with all living beings. Pause.

Breathe in life force. Pause. Exhale connection with all living beings. Pause…

Think of your relationship to your place: in work, your spiritual communities, your family, society, and the cosmos. Think of all the places you may have given away your sense of power to those people or institutions who may wish to control you, or whom you fear, whether for good reasons or bad.

Where have you left your sense of power? Where and when has it been stolen from you? Undermined? Where and when has it been squashed or suppressed?

On each inhalation, begin the process of calling power back.

Call power back from everyone who tried to diminish your strength.

Call power back from any person or institution who told you to fall in line.

Call power back from every person who wanted you to be weak.

Call power back from every time you undermined your own power or made yourself feel weak.

Call power back from force.

Call power back from powerlessness.

Call power back from your fear of being knocked down.

Call power back from perfectionism.

Call back power and your ability to move, act, and do in the world.

Breathe it in.

Expand around it.

Say, "I claim my own strength. I claim my abilities. I claim my autonomy. I claim power."

Fill up with breath. Fill up with the energy of power, whatever that looks or feels like to you.

Keep breathing.

Keep claiming your right to own and share your power.

PASSION

When drawing an invoking pentagram on our bodies, the energy flows from our right hand, down our torso and leg, and into our left foot. We name this point Passion.

Passion is life force aimed toward action. It harnesses both will and intention, as well as body, mind, and emotion, and helps move us forward.

Without passion, it is hard to reach a goal. Passion is desire engaged. Desire itself is important, for it takes our dreams, wants, and wishes, and insists we make them come true. Passion flows from that desire, giving it a large drop of impetus and the slow-building flow of sustainability.

Some of us only think of passion and desire as they relate to physical pleasure, but both words are much more expansive than that.

To desire something is to be willing to take a risk in order to bring it into being.

To have passion is to be willingly engaged in the processes of risk, success, failure, and risk again. Without desire or passion, no risk seems worthwhile, and so we end up in states of non-action.

Non-action is a passive form of risk. Not choosing is a choice.

Passion goads us to choose—something, anything, the thing that we desire—knowing that we may fail to reach our aim, but that damn it, we will keep trying in as many ways we can.

Passion engages our power, our sense of self, and keeps us rooted in our pride. It is in constant conversation with our life force, or sex.

PRACTICE:

I suggest you do some writing to answer the following questions, but you can also meditate on them, make some doodles, or engage with the questions however feels right to you:

When you think of the word passion, what is your first response? Are you excited? Do you feel overwhelmed? Frightened? Emboldened? Filled with life? Afraid to fail? Curious about what lies ahead?

Next: How would you like to shift or deepen your relationship to your own passion?

What might help? More rest? More exercise? More filling the well with art, music, movies, nature, dance?

Do you need to recommit? Or are there ways passion has been knocking at your door that you have ignored?

THE DRIVE TO BE AND DO

Passion is the opposite of both apathy and obsession. Passion helps us welcome our being and embrace our doing in a balanced way.

Without passion, creativity is hard to come by. Without passion, relationships atrophy over time. Friendships and other love relationships become rote. Without passion, justice feels impossible. Without passion, very little that feels important can get done.

Without passion, the world becomes a duller place.

Does this mean we must always feel taken over or carried by the rolling rapids of passion? No. Sometimes passion is a slow and steady stream, other times, those roaring rapids, or a deep, fathomless ocean.

In other words, passion does not always equal intensity, though it can. Especially in the early stages of a project or connection.

Like each of us, passion takes many shapes and forms. It can be quiet or loud, filled with anger or laughter. But passion is the thing that helps us start, continue, and maintain.

If I simply do not care anymore—over a long period of time—it means that passion has dwindled to such a point that I either need to find a way to reengage, or a way to disengage and release.

We will always have periods where engagement feels like a challenge, and depending on our physical health and brain chemistry, we may need support around this. At very least, tracking our levels of passion and engagement offers us greater self-awareness. Awareness helps us decide where to move next.

One question that is useful in assessing our passions is this: "How important is this (relationship, project, goal, work) to me? Am I still willing to put time, energy, effort, and emotion into it even if I need a break right now?"

I try to not make a hard and fast decision when I'm exhausted, for example, or having a bad brain week. But even sitting with those questions is useful. When my brain clears, I can ask again.

Usually, I'll get an answer in my gut. It's like a tugging sense for me that lets me know yes, I still want this. If the answer is no, I might feel a sinking sensation, or uncomfortable tension. As a head-based person, I've learned to listen to my body for confirmation, because it is often more in tune with what I truly desire.

I'm a person whose passions always lead me, but my passions also switch directions, stalling out sometimes and starting anew in a different form. Sometimes my passions are in an ebb because of the vagaries of my autoimmune disorder or my brain dysfunction.

Over the decades, I've noticed that my larger passion cycles tend to run between seven and ten years before something needs to shift. Sometimes these adjustments are minor, other times, they can feel more extreme. Sometimes I find ways to deepen and recommit, and other times, to release.

That's all okay. What matters is I keep finding my ways back to passion. I keep allowing myself different expressions of passion. I keep finding ways to tap the flow, reengage, and swim.

How about you?

. . .

Practice:

What is your current relationship to passion? How often do you feel in the flow? If it helps, write down several categories and assess your engagement or disengagement levels.

Some of these categories might include family, love, sex, creativity, work, health, enjoyment.

Find your own categories. I suggest you begin with three and work your way out from there.

SABOTAGING PASSION

Sometimes we undermine our passions.

It is unfortunately easy to sabotage our relationship to passion—and to our hopes, desires, and dreams—in ways both large and small.

How often do you feel undeserving of going full-out with your passions? Is there a voice asking who are you to be special? Do you feel you need permission from some authority figure or wise friend in order to pursue what you desire? Do you fear getting knocked down if someone notices you?

Do you fear drowning if you take a big risk?

How many times have you been told to be realistic, practical, or to grow up? How many times have you been told that this sort of thing is not for people like you?

Critical voices and fearful patterns enter from many angles, whether we are pursuing creative projects, breaking glass ceilings, insisting on satisfying work, or joining projects linked to social or climate justice.

Some of my critical voices come from my worried, working-class ancestors who would feel more comfortable if I got a regular job. They've had to get used to the fact that isn't going to happen!

Other critical voices come from people I thought were friends, but who—it turns out—wanted companions who maintained a more comfortable status quo.

And one fear pattern comes from a childhood where violence and punishment were random, so staying small felt safer.

How about you? Where do you find these voices or patterns in your life?

We sabotage our passions in other ways, as well. I mentioned status quo, and that is a real thing, both in groups and as individuals. For our purposes, we can also rename that as equilibrium.

EMOTIONAL SET POINTS

Just as people outside us might not want us to rock the boat, we also do that to ourselves.

We all have comfort zones or limits that help us feel safe. Each time we approach the edges of these limits, we tense up, freeze, or flee. Some of us may also fight or fawn as a way to get the sense of comfort back. We have emotional set points and can feel increased discomfort when we hit our usual point.

When we reach the edge of the unknown, we might try to convince ourselves we don't really want or need the thing we were pursuing. We may get sick, or burn some connections or opportunities down. We may come up with a thousand excuses for why the thing won't work, or why it is too much effort, or just a pipe dream.

The reality is, we are most likely afraid. And that's okay. Once we figure out we are afraid, we can do some work on why. But we do not need to wait for that inner work to be done before we decide to dive into our passion anyway.

One gauge I use to assess my responses to expansion and passionate engagement is to notice where I'm holding tension in my body. Another good key is noticing when our breathing grows shallow instead of relaxed and deep. These physical cues are another layer of noticing, and sometimes starting the shift from the physical level helps us more easily work on our emotional and mental patterns.

The good thing is, the set points I'm speaking of are meant to be reset. That does take effort, commitment, and some emotional and mindset work, but it is possible. It is always possible.

Remember the law of inertia: A body at rest stays at rest. A body in motion stays in motion. Flipping our energy and action from rest to motion is a big ask, but passion helps us get there. Like water flowing in a river, passion helps us clear the blocks—or go around them for the moment—and get moving once again.

PRACTICE:

Make a list of all the reasons you can't do the thing, take the risk, open the conversation, or follow your passion.

Then make a list of all the reasons why you really desire the thing, the risk, the conversation, and the passion.

Take your time with this exercise. Notice your physical, mental, and emotional responses to the work. Ponder the list on a walk, or rest with the reasons in a bathtub.

When you need to, pause and slow your breathing down. You can always reengage again.

PASSION AND THE WORLD

Passion helps us engage with our personal wishes and desires, yes, but it also helps us engage with community.

Apathetic, disengaged people are easy to control, subject to the whims and desires of those who hoard money and power. When apathy takes hold, force and oppression rise to meet it, cackling gleefully at how easy their job has become.

The less connected we are to passion, the more easily manipulated we become. Also, we tend to retreat back the energetic and emotional path into a state of powerlessness. Where power and passion feed one another, so do powerlessness and apathy. So do force and obsession.

Just as we must reengage or reassess our connection to personal passions, groups must do the same. Do all members still feel connected to the mission or intention? Is the work still serving that mission or has it veered off course? Does that latter mean the group needs a new mission, or do the strategies and tasks need to shift and come back to focus?

The same is true for more intimate relationships like friendships and romantic, sexual, or work partnerships. What is the intention of the friendship or partnership? Do you even know? What are you and the other person(s) getting from it? What are your intentions toward each other? Have you begun to take your partnership for granted? Do things feel in the flow, or is something damming up the stream?

How do you want to continue to swim together? Or do you want out of the water for now?

If we want to work well together, whether on a creative project, community building, or political action—especially long-term—we require some amount of passion.

Like singers in a choir trading off breaths, the passion level in each person in the collective can ebb and flow.

At one point, you might be one of those filled with the fullness of passion's flow. Then you might need a break, becoming more like a stream, or even a trickle. Others can move in, buoying the group's mission with their passion, until you are ready to surge forth again.

PRACTICE:

How passionate are you about your work with others?

How engaged do others in your group or cadre seem? Do people still feel interested in the project? Are there ways you all might engage and connect even more deeply to your task or mission?

Is it time for the group to refocus or recommit? What might that look like? How would you open that conversation?

Or, if it has been long enough and resistance is too great, is it time for the group to dissolve? Or do you need to personally dissolve your ties, shifting your time, energy, and passion elsewhere?

PART II: THE IRON AND PEARL PENTACLES

CURIOSITY FEEDS PASSION

For me, passion is fed by curiosity.

Think about it: the less curious we are about ourselves, each other, and the world, the less actively engaged we are. We fall into old, familiar patterns, worries, ambitions, or fears.

By invoking curiosity, we allow ourselves to welcome something new. We open ourselves to the unknown, or to possibilities that may currently feel out of reach. Curiosity helps us stretch ourselves, shift direction down half-hidden pathways, and change our ordinary perspective.

What might your connection to passion feel like if you embraced curiosity and the unknown? Would you explore new ways of being in flow with the cosmos? Would you open up different relationships: to humans, to projects, to deities, to magic, to forms of creative expression? Would you welcome more expansive ideas about success, love, justice, health, or community?

Making assumptions or thinking we know something in advance limits possibility, which then curtails or prescribes the boundaries of where our passions can lead us. I'm not speaking of knowing and claiming our expertise or worth here. The people I know who have achieved various levels of mastery remain curious, lifelong. These people continue learning, growing, experimenting, and changing.

So much of our knowledge stems from experience. At first, when things are new, practicing the building blocks to realize our passion can feel challenging and difficult. After some time, we end up incorporating all the required steps, until they become almost as natural as breathing. This is a good thing.

This embodiment of our skills, talents, or craft can also lead to doing things by rote. In many relationships, this can also lead to making assumptions. We stop asking. We cease to engage. Passion dries up when we aren't curious anymore.

To invoke curiosity is to remain connected. This includes successful, long-term relationships, whether one-on-one or in community.

True experts, and people who have longevity of practice, are eternally curious, always returning to "what if?"

Yes. What if? That phrase alone is a marvelous way to invoke curiosity and re-engage passion, creativity, magic, and desire.

CALLING BACK PASSION

Whether you feel in the flow of passion now or not, there are likely times it has felt like passion has fled.

How often have you given up on passion?

How often have you thought that passion was for other people, but not for you?

When has your passion felt depleted by overwork, or exhaustion, or illness, or depression?

When has passion felt distant and out of reach?

Like all the points on the Iron Pentacle, we can call back and reclaim Passion. Let's do this.

PRACTICE:

Read this through as many times as you need to before

engaging with this exercise. Remember, you are the one in charge here.

Breathe in life force. Pause. Exhale connection with all living beings. Pause.

Breathe in life force. Pause. Exhale connection with all living beings. Pause.

Breathe in life force. Pause. Exhale connection with all living beings. Pause...

Think of your life as it is now. Notice your sense of passion. Remember the times when passion felt overwhelming or suppressed.

Where did you leave your connection to passion? How often has passion been derided, laughed at, or scorned?

On each inhalation, begin the process of calling passion back.

Call passion back from everyone who tried to tell you what you desired was ridiculous or useless.

Call passion back from any person or institution who wants you to remain docile and quiet.

Call passion back from every instance of uncertainty or fear.

Call passion back from every situation that tried to block your flow.

Call passion back from apathy.

Call passion back from obsession.

Call passion back.

Breathe it in.

Expand around it.

Say, "I claim my own passion. I claim my hopes, dreams,

and desires. I claim my energy. I claim passion for myself and for the greater good."

Fill up with breath. Fill up with the energy of passion, whatever that looks or feels like to you.

Keep breathing.

Keep claiming your right to the energy and flow of passion.

THE CYCLE CONTINUES

And so Passion cycles back to Sex, and then a sunwise circle moves from Sex, to Self, to Passion, to Pride, to Power. This sunwise circle balances these energies within us, and in the world.

We can think of the lines connecting the points in the star shape as helping to cleanse and activate the energies. The sunwise circle seals these qualities into our energy field and our physical, psychic, and emotional space, steering us toward better health and balance.

When our life force feeds our sense of self, we can grow in healthy, generative ways. When our self connects with passion, our work in the world becomes more clear. Living engaged with passion, we can find our pride, taking our place in the world. From a place of pride, we enter the realm of balanced power, connected to community, to the elements, and then reaching back to the flow of life force, and to sex.

With all of that said, I'd like to return for a moment to what happens when this outer circle runs in an anti-sunwise direction.

Read this sequence and notice how it feels in your body: Sex, Power, Pride, Passion, Self.

Now think about how things run in society at large. For me, that sequence feels out of balance and causes tension in my gut.

In dominant society, when life force moves directly into power before being tempered by the energies of the other points, things tend to go awry. We end up with oppression, greed, oligarchy, authoritarianism, and abuse. We end up with individuals who only want power-over at the cost of everything else.

That power-over then bolsters arrogance instead of healthy pride, giving rise to passions that are often better left unplumbed. What sense of self arises from this sequence? There are many variations, and none of them feel good to me.

We do not have to live this way.

We can, instead, seek out greater harmony and equanimity, enlivened by the qualities of the Iron Pentacle in our quest to become more human.

What does it mean to become more human? For me, that means seeking wholeness and flow with everything around me. It means reflecting what is and envisioning what could be.

To become more human is to become better suited to our environment, from the soil beneath our feet to the most distant of stars.

When we invoke and reclaim the powers of Sex, Pride, Self, Power, and Passion, we forge a spell.

What might that spell become?

PART II: THE IRON AND PEARL PENTACLES

I encourage you to go back and read the opening section, where we ran the pentacle through our bodies, from Sex to Pride to Self to Power to Passion to Sex. Then take a breath, and feel the sunwise circle activate: Sex, Self, Passion, Pride, Power, Sex.

We are human. We are beautiful. We are varied.

We are whole.

We follow the pathway of the sun as it moves across the earth.

We invoke ourselves, fully human, dancing with the cycles of life.

THE PEARL PENTACLE

Pearls are made of the grit of life. A small irritation. A grain of sand.

The mollusk secretes nacre—calcium carbonate and protein—around the irritation, building the pearl, layer upon layer, making something beautiful, lustrous, and smooth where once there was only pain.

We can do the same. We take the stuff of life, and surround it with spiritual practice, with music, with community, with joy. Over time, the irritation and pain become shining things of beauty, and life continues.

Think of the pearls built by you in your lifetime so far. Think of the pearls formed within community.

So many artists, parents, activists, and teachers have passed along this lesson of building beauty from pain.

I think of the Theater of the Oppressed, in which Brazilian Augusto Boal and his actors led community members to craft theater from the harsh conditions of their lived experience, with the purpose to transform that reality into something new.

This in turn, was inspired by educator Paulo Freire's *Pedagogy of the Oppressed*, which was written as a counterpoint to educational systems in which the oppressors held the upper hand. Freire believed oppressed people could wrest back education for themselves, becoming agents of change.

I think also of revolutionary Emma Goldman, wishing for "freedom, the right to self-expression, everybody's right to beautiful, radiant things." In this way, her politics was grounded in joy. She worked tirelessly for justice, while insisting on a deep appreciation of life.

There are thousands of examples like this throughout

history. They show us that, where there is strife, we can find moments of harmony. Where there is despair, hope lives, too. Even in the most harrowing of times, humans have managed to find moments of beauty, love, and care. Humans have managed to care for each other and foster the creative spark.

Over the forty years I have studied and worked with the Pearl Pentacle, I've returned to this lesson, over and over. It is not always easy, but for longevity's sake, I have found it necessary to pause, and remember why I am alive, and to notice all the ways the lives of others touch mine.

And then I see the patterns we paint together. And once again, I invoke the transformative power of pearl.

INVOKING PEARL

We invoke the luminous beauty of the pearl. We invoke the shimmering of the moon and stars above our heads. We invoke our humanity, as it connects into community.

We invoke the power of Love, the strength of an open, connected heart.

We invoke the power of Law, of living in right relationship with the flow of nature.

We invoke the power of Knowledge, both personal and collective.

We invoke the power of Liberty, of the freedom that comes from claiming the power we have with each other and within ourselves.

We invoke the power of Wisdom. which flows from our engagement with our passions.

We invoke the Pearl.

Practice:

Note: if you live in the Southern Hemisphere and feel more comfortable shifting this so clockwise and counter-clockwise are correct for you, please feel free.

Stand or lie down, with enough room to arrange your arms and legs into a star position. If your body is not able to do this, get as comfortable as possible, and know that you can run energy both through your physical body and toward a star shape around your physical body.

If you are standing, you can lower your arms whenever you need to, and raise them again as you have the energy or strength to do so.

Let us begin.

Slow your breathing down. Connect with your center, that place of stillness between your navel and your pelvis. Breathe into center.

Imagine a pearl forming in an oyster beneath the sea. Now hold in your mind's eye the pearl shape of the full moon above your head, luminous and glowing. Breathe. Notice the connection between the pearl in the mollusk clinging to an ocean rock, and the moon above. Feel how those connect through you, through the grit and beauty of your life.

As you inhale, draw down the pearlescent light from the moon, and fill your body with that energy. As you exhale, connect with the pearl forming in the sea. Repeat this until you've established a rhythm and a connection: heart of the

PART II: THE IRON AND PEARL PENTACLES

moon, center of your body, heart of the sea, return. Heart of the moon, center of your body, heart of the sea, return. Heart of the moon, center of your body, heart of the sea, return.

Now, imagine that pearlescent energy forming itself into a small ball inside your head, somewhere behind your third eye or pineal gland.

Feel it glowing, luminous, there. Name that point Love.

Now, imagine that white pearl energy flowing down your body, forming a small ball in your right foot.

Feel it illuminated there. Name that point Law.

Now, imagine that white pearl energy flowing up your body, forming a small ball in your left hand.

Feel it glowing there. Name that point Knowledge.

Now, imagine that white pearl energy flowing across your body, forming a small ball in your right hand.

Feel it glowing there. Name that point Liberty.

Now, imagine that white pearl energy flowing down your body, forming a small ball in your left foot.

Feel it glowing there. Name that point Wisdom.

Now, imagine that white pearl energy flowing back up your body, back to the small ball in your head. Name that point Love.

Pause a moment here and breathe awhile. Notice all the points: Love, Law, Knowledge, Liberty, Wisdom. Notice how your energy forms a star.

Keep connecting with, and relaxing into, your breath.

Now, imagine a sunwise circle being traced around your body, from Love, to Knowledge, to Wisdom, to Law, to Liberty, and back to Love.

Keep breathing. Notice how you feel. Notice the possibility in this form. Your form. Your life. Your luminous beauty.

Notice the possibility of this energy, flowing toward community, bathing everyone you love, washing everything that you hold dear.

Are you ready to continue?

LOVE

The Pearl Pentacle begins and ends with Love. If we are mapping a star onto our physical bodies, the energy of Love resides in our head, singing with the energy of Sex.

If Iron helps us work on self, Pearl helps us work in and with community. Without some basis in love, community is hard to foster. If sex is raw energy and the stuff of life, so is love.

Victor Anderson used to say that the Iron and Pearl Pentacles were the same notes, played one octave apart. So let's think of sex and love that way. Both are fueled by, affirm, and foster life. One way to wrap our heads around this is to think of sex as the individual connection of a single bee with one flower and love as the community connection of a hive to a whole, colorful field.

For me, love makes up the fabric of the universe. It is the great connector, linking stars to cells, atoms to galaxies. We are each small cells in this larger body. We are threads in the tapestry. Notes within the song. And with each other, linked in purpose through the power of love, we become cell clusters, patterns within the fabric, a bass line or melody within the song.

We each bring our own sense of connection to life into all of our other relationships. Family—found, chosen, or by birth—becomes imbued with this drop of life that only we can bring. So does our temple, coven, church, workplace, mutual aid group, and circle of friends.

No connection is exactly the same, and in concert, all of our connections can create a melody. Disconnection creates disharmony. We hear it, see it, and feel it in our muscles and our bones. Whereas the music of connectivity fills us with warmth, inspiration, or courage, the music of disconnection fills us with angst or dread.

Love. Not love. Love. Not love. Assessing which is which requires our presence and a developing awareness of how our relationships make us *feel*.

Love offers health. Not love offers dis-ease.

WHAT IS LOVE?

Love emerges from sex, from life force, from the energy of creation. Love is the great connector, the energy that links all living things together.

Love flows through touch. Conversation. Acts of service. Love flows through music and dance, story and art. Love shares. Love galvanizes us into action. Love invites us into rest.

Love exists in the space between each molecule and the distance between stars.

Love sparks anger at injustice. Love fosters creativity. Love is gentle. Love courts possibility. Love draws boundaries. Love opens doors.

If love includes all of these, then what in the world does the word even mean? And how does something like a boundary foster greater connection?

Thinking about sex and love as connectors offers us the biggest clue. Without access to sex—life force—and love, we have a tendency to go inert. To rely on default and non-action. Laughter is hollow. Food does not taste as good. We aren't filled with a sense of joy and comfort at the scent of bread baking or roses blooming by the sidewalk's edge. Even the act of sex itself becomes mechanical, or an exercise in control rather than a coming together of two equal beings.

For me, love is not only connection, but also immanent, permeating all things in the cosmos.

A boundary drawn by love enables healthier relationships. Anger fueled by love brings change. When I cut myself off from the flow of love, forgetting my connection with all living beings, I diminish my ability to live, and to live well.

The more I embrace love, the more easily life flows within, around, and through me. Love connects me to the community of this planet and our connection to the moon, sun, and stars.

LOVE IS GREATER THAN FEAR

If love is the great connector, the absence of love brings disconnection. Fear.

Decades ago—during one round of the US war with Iraq—I used to sit in meditation outside the San Francisco Federal

Building with a sign that read Love > Fear. I still hold that message to be true.

The more we live in fear, the more our connection to love constricts. There are those in the world that want nothing more than for whole groups of us to live in fear, because, in sundering our connections with each other, they increase their power over us all. This especially holds true for any groups the overculture is intent on making marginalized.

When actively oppressed groups insist on art, beauty, community care, and mutual aid, love triumphs. These communities survive, resilient against the onslaught of corruption, abuse, and pain.

Think of one single abused human. If they can find connection with one other being, their odds for survival and eventual healing increase. This connection might be with an animal, a plant, a book, or a song. Think of people who survived torture because they were able to recite sonnets in their heads. Think of children who make it through because of a stuffed animal, a pet cat, or a single friend.

We are made to love, no matter how often the world may try to tell us otherwise. Love reminds us that we need one another, not only to survive, but to thrive.

Love exists in the simplest of actions and encounters. Love is in the smile to the passerby. Love is in the dandelion growing in the sidewalk cracks. Love is in the kind word, the cup of coffee, the listening ear. Love exists when a group of people surround their neighbor to protect them from detention by fascists. Love exists when someone speaks up in support of a coworker, friend, or child.

Love makes us stronger. More resilient. Better able to show up for the fight. Love offers rest and respite, beauty and joy.

Love is the great connector. Love is always stronger than fear.

BOUNDARIES AND LOVE

At its most expansive, love is boundless. It reaches past the stars. Linked with the spirit that enlivens, love flows in and around all things.

But love also sets boundaries when necessary. It contains. It lends structure. It directs the flow of life.

Think of a time when you felt unsafe? What did—or might have—brought a sense of safety to the situation? Sometimes that is a clear, healthy boundary. A safe place. Encircling arms. The word "no."

Other times, boundaries might feel restrictive. Smothering. Too confining. Those boundaries are not the boundaries set by love. Instead, those are boundaries made out of fear, or from a wish to control.

Can you feel the difference in your body? In your emotions? In your energy field?

I certainly can. It took me years to learn healthy boundaries because the only boundaries I knew were those set by fear or control. I'm still learning and growing in my relationship with boundaries set by love, and likely will be until the last breath leaves my lungs.

In speaking of boundaries and love, I like to think of the banks of a river. The banks move and shift along with the water, often traveling for miles on either side, snaking along the surface of the earth. But that does not make the boundaries any less helpful. The earthy banks and the river speak with one another—when they are allowed to—and the land grows rich from this dance of love. In turn, the people who live nearby benefited from this fecundity and wealth.

When some humans finally set boundaries upon the river and its banks, we did so in an attempt to control. That often goes awry, as anyone who lives near a flood plane can attest.

So, the paradox is that love is both limitless and bounded. We need both possibilities in order to grow into ourselves.

You can shape your relationship to love as the river and its earthen banks shape each other.

Practice:

What areas of your life could use firmer boundaries? How might you set those boundaries—for yourself and others—from a place of respect and love?

Ponder this for a while. Write some things down. Walk with the question, or sleep on it.

What areas of your life could use looser boundaries? What adjustments might you make to let more love in?

When do you feel connected to a sense of boundlessness and expansion? How does that make you feel? Is it exciting? Exhilarating? Terrifying? Does the thought of boundless love and life cause you to feel overwhelmed, or do you wish to expand along with it?

There are no right answers to any of my questions here. I encourage you to take a deep breath and return to these questions, again and again.

PART II: THE IRON AND PEARL PENTACLES

THE THINGS WE LOVE

One morning, after lighting my candles and making my prayers, I decided to focus on the things I love.

Why? Because times felt very hard. It was easy to get trapped in the maelstrom of terrible news. Times might feel hard for you as you read these words, too. Maybe you're going through something close to home that weighs you down. Perhaps world events feel overwhelming. Or maybe your brain or body is just having one of those days.

Returning to a practice of love, and focusing on that, helps me regain some equilibrium, as well as the ability to act instead of curling up in a ball and hiding. So, it becomes my practice to remember love. This is not papering over the bad and calling it love. This is not the toxic positivity or spiritual bypassing of ignoring injustice and responding with "love and light."

No. Sometimes, as Dostoevsky once wrote, love in reality is a harsh and dreadful thing compared to love in dreams.

Love is the reason the cruelty makes me angry and gets me down. Love is the reason injustice requires a response. Love is the reason I do what I do, day in and day out. Love is why I keep showing up. It bolsters and inspires me. It fuels my rage and my tears. Love opens my heart to the world and helps me greet it, once again.

I love and appreciate so many things about my life and this world. There are people whom I love. Chance moments. The moon in the night sky. A song in my ears. Squirrels chasing around a tree. A mourning dove at the birdbath. Stickers on signposts. A good cup of tea. The fall of camellia petals on a blue recycling bin.

Love exists. Love imbues this world. And some days, that is enough.

Bernice King—and many others—link justice and love, and I think that is correct. She wrote: "Justice is Love lived out. Justice isn't revenge, it's re/alignment with Love. Justice re/aligns culture with Love. Justice re/aligns the climate with Love. Justice re/aligns policies with Love. Justice holds institutions accountable for Love. Justice is love we can witness."

I appreciate this reminder the love is powerful. Love is not avoidance or suppression. Love confronts the world as it is and helps us grow in better alignment with healthier, more compassionate forms of what could be.

TUNE IN TO YOUR HEART

Take a deep breath. Notice your body. How do you feel? Are you tired? Jumpy? Energized? Agitated? Exhausted?

All of the above?

Take another deep breath.

How is your emotional state? Do you feel lonely? Fearful? Happy? Anxious? Empowered? The answer to that question will vary, person to person and day to day, because the possibilities are so personal, always.

Some of us are alone. Some of us are caretakers. Some of us need care. Some of us are caregivers who also need care. Some of us are busy. Some don't feel busy enough. Some of us feel solid and steady, ready to face what each day brings. Others of us may wish to crawl back into bed.

All of this, in the midst of world events, affects our emotional states, or what we call our hearts.

The physical heart is a muscle, of course. And muscles can feel strong or weak, vital or weary. Battered, bruised, or well cared for. As I write these words, I've recommitted to getting more physical exercise as an act of love. It is love toward myself and my body, but it is also love toward community and creativity.

I want my heart and body to be as healthy as possible, even within the aging process and my autoimmune disorder.

I want to live to love another day. To remain in the good fight. To spread what love I can to as few or many are around to receive it.

And I want to remain open to receive love myself. To keep connecting. We are in this life together, us and our hearts.

So, notice your body. Notice your emotions. What might offer you better support right now?

What helps you take care of your heart?

PRACTICE:

Take a deep breath. Drop your attention to that space high up within your protective ribs. Place a hand there. Lightly tap your breastbone with your fingertips or the heel of you hand.

Keep breathing, deep and slow. Let the tapping release any excess tension you may feel. Imagine it floating or draining away.

Gently focus your attention on the area of your physical heart as you breathe and tap.

You can stop the tapping at any point that feels right.

As you do this practice, tune in. What does your heart need today? What is one way you can offer your heart what it needs?

RECLAIMING LOVE

Like sex, love gets blocked and twisted by the overculture. The overculture uses the word love to describe toxic, fearful behavior. Jealousy is equated to love. Controlling behavior is linked to love. Neediness and desperation are branded as expressions of love.

None of these are love. They are simply jealousy, controlling, neediness, or desperation.

"But Thorn," you might reply, "didn't you say sometimes your anger arises from love?"

Yes. But not all anger does. Anger is anger. Love is love. Love can fuel anger, but so can hatred or the wish to hold power over another.

Our sense of love, like our sense of connection, belongs to us, just as our personal link to sex and life force does. Life energy, as expressed through both sex and love, should never be under the control of someone else. Consent equals respect, and both love and sex thrive where respect is present.

Disrespect shrivels love, no matter what it is called. We must be free to love as we will, without coercion, and without coercing another.

Healthy human beings reclaim the power of love for the good of themselves and others.

We can call back our connection to life force, to creativity, to connection, to love.

We can claim the love point for ourselves and our lives, for the good of community, and the safekeeping of this world, and all the worlds.

Shall we practice?

PART II: THE IRON AND PEARL PENTACLES

. . .

PRACTICE:

Read this through as many times as you need to before engaging with this exercise. If you find yourself constricting, slow down your breathing. Exhale on a sigh, and imagine you can relax your edges.

But regardless of our current relationship to the point of love, I encourage us all to try. Some of us may just need more time.

Breathe in life force. Pause. Exhale connection with all living beings. Pause.

Breathe in life force. Pause. Exhale connection with all living beings. Pause.

Breathe in life force. Pause. Exhale connection with all living beings. Pause...

Think of your relationship to connection, to your body, to creativity, to life, and to what we call love. Think of all the places you may have given away your autonomy in this realm.

Where have you left your love? Where and when has it been stolen from you? Where and when has love felt squashed, twisted, demanded, or suppressed?

On each inhalation, begin the process of calling love back.

Call love back from everyone who tried to control you against your will.

Call love back from whomever told you that you were not loveable.

Call love back from any person or institution who told you certain people were not deserving of love.

Call love back from every friend or lover you've ever had.

Call love back from every person you thought you were loving, but who could not or would not love you back.

Call love back from moments of coercion or nonconsensual dominance.

Call love back from violence.

Call love back from disapproval.

Call love back from fear.

Call love back from every heartbreak, each disappointment, every time you gave up.

Call love back.

Breathe it in.

Expand around it.

Say, "I claim connection. I claim my spirit's connection to the flow of life. I claim my relationship to love."

Fill up with life. Fill up with the energy of love, whatever that looks or feels like to you.

Keep breathing.

Keep claiming your connection to the power of love.

LAW

When we draw an invoking pentagram on our bodies, the energy flows from the head to our right foot. We name this point Law. It sings with the energy of Pride.

To live with law is to live in tune with the cycles of nature. To live with law is to recognize our internal authority and the ways in which that can mesh with the sovereignty of others.

Remember the boundlessness and boundaries of love? Law reflects both of those states, taking and transmuting that energy into one of shifting balance.

Law sets strong boundaries and shows what happens when boundlessness occurs, sometimes in direct response to lack of boundaries. Think of human-wrought climate shifts. The responses in nature from that lack of a boundary is shown when boundaries are breached, often catastrophically.

Law is connected to personal and collective will. Like a

blade forged in fire, and coupled with our intention, law helps us move in the world with purpose and grace.

We must uncouple our relationship to law from our encounters with legislation or so-called systems of justice. It is far more useful to think of the cycles of nature that we are part of, even those of us who feel alienated from them by our dependence on clock time and electricity, central heating and cooling, and the pressures of human life.

The less in tune we are with natural cycles and the less interested we are in ethics as opposed to morals, the more we require things like legislation. We can change this.

Ethics, like Law, require relationship with everything around us. Ethics invites us to make decisions based on current reality, including something as simple as obeying a stop sign in order to increase community safety levels.

To live as an ethical person requires us to be open to the power of Love. It requires us to take responsibility for our place in the world, invoking that resonating octave of Pride and Law.

Law naturally arises from the connectivity of Love. Law sings in harmony with Pride. If Pride helps us know our place in the world, Law opens us to a richer comprehension of what this means. When we live in concert with the forces of nature, rather than in constant states of opposition and control, our sense of pride increases. So does our ability to work with others —be those others human, animal, fruit, or insect.

We also increase our ability to harmonize with all the worlds, seen and unseen.

Law brings us closer to wholeness.

PART II: THE IRON AND PEARL PENTACLES

WHAT IS LAW?

Law is the sun combusting.

Law is the Gulf Stream sending water traveling vast distances.

Law is meteorites sparking in the sky.

Law is an earthquake releasing pressure from a fault line.

Law is fire cutting through a forest to thin the groundcover and spread seeds.

Law is a honeybee, gathering pollen and returning to the hive.

Law is an ant drinking water from a cupped leaf after the rain.

Law is the river, shifting in its banks, bringing fertile muck to grace the land.

Law is compost and decay feeding new life.

To comprehend Law is to develop a deeper understanding of the way the sun combusts and helps vegetation on this spinning planet we call home to grow. Understanding Law helps us tune our emotions and thoughts to the phases of the moon and the shifting of tides. Understanding Law roots us in the changing of seasons, whether subtle or extreme.

There are laws of gravity. Laws of thermodynamics. Laws of expansion and contraction. Laws of inertia.

If matter and energy can neither be created nor destroyed, Law reminds us that some part of us is eternal.

If a body at rest stays at rest, and a body in motion stays in motion, we can tap into the laws of inertia to help get us moving once again, perhaps increasing our sense of purpose and bolstering our pride.

As we are part of nature, we are also part of Law.

LAW AND THE SELF

If we aren't speaking of legislation, how does Law affect us as individuals?

I saw Law in action as a child when riding my bicycle down a steep hill. Too small and slight to control the metal beast at such a high speed, my bike got the wobbles and I was thrown to the ground, scraping my knees. I encountered both gravity and physics that day. My respect for both only increased.

Aging is another way we encounter Law. As we are part of nature, we are subject to time, to gravity, to the effects of sun, wind, and cold. Our bodies change in accordance with these patterns.

We can invoke other facets of Law to influence the rate of these changes but cannot stop them. Accepting that helps us live in greater harmony, blending the energy of both Pride and Law.

Law also helps us to act ethically with each other, shifting our relationships toward greater health. We'll speak more of that shortly.

If I have developed a balanced sense of Pride, Law becomes my friend and ally. When I know my value, and have taken my place in the world, I can then expand my sense of both boundaries and responsibility. This enables me to live in accordance with my will, part of the cycles of Law.

Practice:

Sit in meditation, or take a walk, or journal and ponder your personal relationship with Law. What effects do you see that Law has on your life? How in tune are you with the cycles around you?

What changes might you make to clarify or strengthen your connection to Law?

LAW AND TIME

How is Law reflected in the communities we build? How are our guidelines set in accordance with ethics, inclusion, and a connection to the planet itself?

The energy of Law—not legislation—helps me in my quest to live more ethically. The more I notice my relationships with the world around me, the less harm my action or inaction might cause over time. I can adjust myself to reflect these relationships, deepening my connections over time.

Speaking of time: acknowledging my part in the larger flow of cycles reminds me of my place in the cosmos. Yes, I have effect right now, but I am also part of a longer arc, be that ten thousand or one hundred thousand years.

Therefore, as with Pride, Law reminds me of who and where I am in the scheme of things. I personally find this reflection to be comforting. It means I don't have to get everything right. Nor am I responsible for the turning of these cycles on my own. I am simply part of them. One tiny, minuscule part.

I am both important and insignificant, and that feels just fine.

That's large scale, but what about small?

I'll get to that next.

LAW, RELATIONSHIP, AND GOOD FAITH

Using ethical relationship as our guide, we can invoke the power of Law in our families, friend groups, and other communities. As a leftist, it is my hope and desire that the more we do this closer in, the more this sort of Law has a chance to ripple out, one community affecting another, and so on, until whole towns and cities are involved in the dance.

Even small countries, provinces, or states can get on board, deciding to house people instead of punishing them. Deciding to offer free schooling and support instead of prisons. Deciding that a working-class neighborhood is more important than a highway. Deciding that the old growth forest is more important than the wood pulp it provides.

None of this is a pipe dream. There are thousands of examples we can point to that are working right now.

So where do we begin? We begin in the circles of relationship closer in.

How many disagreements might be worked through if we paid broader attention to each other, and tried to understand context and motivation before drawing conclusions about intention?

What if we treated one another with good faith?

The assumption of bad faith poisons every interaction it touches. I have been the recipient of bad faith, not comprehending it until I realized everything I said or did was being misread because of an earlier miscommunication. It's not a pretty thing to experience.

Bad faith arguments run half of Internet discourse, stifling the exchange of ideas.

I'm not saying we shouldn't be on guard against bad faith actors, of whom there are many. But especially with people we want to work with? If we don't begin with an assumption of good faith, we'll get nowhere fast.

How often do we work to undermine each other, rather than support one another toward the common good? This sort of behavior ruins many communities, workplaces, and projects. It usually arises from insecurity or jockeying for power-over. This denotes a lack of true pride.

Lack of true Pride—and of knowing and claiming our place in community—undermines Law.

In working with community, we work on ourselves, and vice versa.

ETHICS VS. MORALS

Ethics, as I've said, are rooted in relationships. They can shift as our understanding deepens. This is different from what we often call morals. Morality can become a box into which we try to shove every situation. It does not require us to be in active relationship at all.

Both ethics and morals can reflect our values, but I find it easier to actually live out my stated values with ethical relationship as my guide. Morality can whitewash over actual action with stated beliefs that may be in direct conflict with those actions. With ethics, that is not possible. To act ethically requires belief and action to work together.

Now, we can have a strong moral code that is the backbone of our ethics, but that is more like our spine enabling our skeleton to move freely, rather than bringing everything into lockstep formation.

Also, morals are most often something imposed from outside of us, by institutions or strong social pressure.

A well-grounded, centered ethics reclaims our power from these institutions and helps us become autonomous beings. Ethics allows us to reflect and then act in a way that feels most compassionate and true. We will see these qualities reflected later, in the Pentacle of Autonomy.

Striving to live ethically means I must consistently return to center, assess my values, and then act in relationship with what is in front of or around me.

Practice:

What is your relationship with ethics? What is your history with morals and morality?

Is there something you need to reassess or shake off? Are there changes—large or small—you can make to bring yourself into greater alignment with your values?

What are some ways you put your values into action?

RECLAIMING LAW

In a world where prisons, courts, and war are thought to enact law and bring about justice, how do we reclaim the energy of Law?

Like the concept of pride, law is too often used to punish and oppress, bringing life further and further out of balance, rather than into balance.

One entry point to shift this for me comes from the ancient Egyptian concept of Ma'at, named after the Goddess of that name. Her attributes include such qualities as harmony, balance, justice, reciprocity, and order.

I often invoke justice in this way, both as a blessing and a curse. Leveling justice at oligarchs and other oppressors is a favored curse of mine, especially since those people all too often use the blunt force of what the overculture calls law to punish those with fewer resources.

So, to reclaim Law is to begin to cleanse our own thoughts, opinions, and actions away from that sort of punitive legislation and toward the balance, justice, and reciprocity seen in Ma'at.

We can reclaim the power of Law as a way to unchain ourselves and our communities from the ubiquity of punishment. In this way, the power of Law can become as simple as feeding someone or planting a tree.

We can reclaim Law as a force of relationship and harmony with each other, life here on earth, and with the cosmos itself.

We can invoke Law as a pattern we weave together.

Shall we practice?

PRACTICE:

Read this through as many times as you need to before engaging with this exercise. As usual, if you find yourself constricting, slow down your breathing. Exhale on a sigh, and imagine you can relax your edges.

Some of us may need to ease into this practice, depending

on our personal, community, or ancestral relationship to the concept of law.

But regardless, I encourage us all to try. Some of us may just need more time.

Breathe in life force. Pause. Exhale connection with all living beings. Pause.

Breathe in life force. Pause. Exhale connection with all living beings. Pause.

Breathe in life force. Pause. Exhale connection with all living beings. Pause...

Think of your relationship to reciprocity, to community, to justice, to harmony, to time and tides. Think of your place in the cosmos. Think of Law. Think of all the places you may have given away your agency around this.

Where has the twisted version of law been used against you? Where and when has healthy, integrated Law been stolen from you? Where and when has Law felt like punishment and oppression?

On each inhalation, begin the process of calling Law back.

Call Law back from everyone who tried to control you against your will.

Call Law back from whomever told you that you deserved punishment.

Call Law back from any person or institution who told you certain people were not deserving of justice or respect.

Call Law back from your resistance to the flow of time. Call Law back from your fear or death or aging. Call Law back.

Call Law back from moments of overweening privilege and harsh judgement.

Call Law back from violence.

Call Law back from the police.
Call Law back from the prisons and courts.
Call Law back from petty, punitive action.
Call Law back.
Breathe it in.
Expand around it.

Say, "I claim relationship. I claim my spirit's connection to the flow of harmony and natural law. I claim my relationship to Law itself."

Fill up with life. Fill up with the energy of Law, whatever that looks or feels like to you.

Keep breathing.

Keep claiming your connection to the power of Law.

KNOWLEDGE

The pentacle continues, the energy tracing a path up toward our left hand, invoking Knowledge.

Knowledge is rooted in Self, and the power of Air. Self is required to assimilate and comprehend data and information, whether that comes from our senses, or via our intellect. In this way, Knowledge is holistic. Without the ability to parse and connect information, we cannot say we have Knowledge.

This is true communally, as well. We have collective sources of data and information that filter through our experiences and history both as individuals and a group. Together, we transmute this into Knowledge, increasing the effectiveness of the group mind.

The incorporation of Knowledge allows us to adapt as necessary, making it easier to embrace necessary change, rather than being forced into change or digging in our heels in refusal, stagnating and stultifying our individual and collective mores. This is not to say that Knowledge always brings change. Other times, Knowledge enables us to commit more thoroughly to what is, and what has been.

Knowledge is not something static that we cling to. Knowledge, like air, flows.

Also, like air, Knowledge is helped by openness. When Knowledge becomes stuck in an enclosed system, it degrades and begins to twist in upon itself, until it loses its ability to take on any new insight or information. When this happens, the system itself must fracture and crack. Sometimes these fracture points offer enough space for new ideas and information to flow through. Other times? The entire structure must fall into wreckage.

On both an individual and collective level, that complete collapse can be extremely painful, and sometimes psychically—or even physically—dangerous. But that does not mean it isn't sometimes necessary, despite how terrible the process feels, or what the consequences may be.

We see this in social, political, and economic systems built by humans. Dictatorships rise and fall. Economic systems fail. Brittle ideologies will do everything within their power to sustain themselves until they simply cannot anymore. Or until the people suffering within them rise up and say, "No more."

What does all of that have to do with Knowledge? At least partially, all of those systems are built upon definitions of Self and Knowledge that end up serving the few. We'll examine more of how this works when we get to Liberty.

Let me offer a smaller example. In my late twenties, I returned to university to finally get a degree. I'd dropped out high school at sixteen, and college not long after. Why? Those places were not where the knowledge I sought was found. But finally, with some life experience behind me, I longed to study in a structured way again.

Entering university, I studied for a degree I still use every day: Philosophy and Religion.

Studying gave me a richer understanding of the ways in which knowledge both expands and contracts us as human beings. I read philosophers who reached beyond what their Self had already incorporated, in an attempt to know still more.

I also read philosophers whose theories became that closed system I touched on earlier. They followed their own theories into tighter and tighter spirals, with complete consistency, until they painted themselves into a tiny hole they could not crawl out of.

They sought no outside input, relying instead only on the power of their own minds. Their minds were prodigious, and their philosophies made sense as long as they remained untouched by the outside world.

You see, these philosophies—though beautiful, engaging, and sometimes even convincing—were also broken. They lacked the flow of air and the openness of curiosity to the world around them. Air is not consistent. Self changes over time, or we hope it does. In order to remain relevant, so must Knowledge.

WHAT IS KNOWLEDGE?

What is Knowledge?
Knowledge is understanding.
Knowledge is comprehension.

PART II: THE IRON AND PEARL PENTACLES

Knowledge is assimilated skill or information, gained from learning and placed in context.

When we place information in context, our relationship to it changes. We cannot say we know something until we have incorporated it somehow, whether that is within ourselves, our group, or simply within the context I'm speaking of.

Context includes other data points. Context includes the world around us. Context includes the information we draw in through our senses. Context includes other facets and angles of knowledge, too.

So Knowledge, like all the other points on the Iron and Pearl pentacles, does not exist in a vacuum. Just like life itself.

Knowledge may begin with theory, but is not only theory.

Knowledge may begin with information, but is not only information.

Knowledge may be backed up by data, but it is not only data.

Knowledge, via Self, requires experience in order to flourish. Knowledge, in this way, is information applied.

We cannot learn without opening ourselves to the world or to our inner depths.

The roots of the word knowledge come from "to acknowledge" or, in other words, to recognize. To encounter. To see. So here we are, back to relationship again.

A stream of data is meaningless if we don't know how to read it. Information is just a collection of facts without meaning. Relationship to data and information, coupled with experience and context, leads to understanding.

To claim Knowledge is to recognize a part of ourselves, reflected in the world.

• • •

PRACTICE:

What is your definition of Knowledge and how does it operate in your life?

Take a pen and paper, and set a timer for ten minutes. Write at the top: "Knowledge is..."

See what comes out as the pen moves, teasing out your thoughts onto paper.

When it feels right, shift to writing "I know..."

When you are done, read what you've written and reflect upon it.

How true does what you've written feel?

KNOW THYSELF

Every seeker wishing to consult with the Oracle of Delphi had to pass beneath an archway inscribed with the words "Know Thyself."

Why? Well, self-knowledge is the key to gnosis, which is sometimes defined as the knowledge of esoteric, or spiritual truths. The origins of the word gnosis also include awareness. Awareness brings us back to our senses, and a connection to the world around us, including the worlds unseen.

The other reason the oracle commanded the seekers to know themselves was this: without self-knowledge, divination and oracular utterances are meaningless. Without self-knowledge, we don't have the tools or skills to apply any wisdom the oracle might impart.

The same can be said, I think, for any form of study. To truly understand a concept, or how something works—let alone to plumb the mysteries of mathematics, physics, or philosophy—we must bring ourselves to bear upon the problem in front of us.

To know myself is to begin to know the world. If I know myself, I can more easily understand the workings of a steam engine, a computer, or a worker-owned collective.

If this sounds strange to you, pause a moment. If the workings of yourself are opaque to you, how does that affect all your relationships? If we don't know ourselves, how can we expect to truly understand anything outside of ourselves?

When I look back on relationships I had when I was younger—romance, friendships, with dance troupes, or covens, or political action collectives—I can see now the ways in which I was missing key pieces of information about myself. So, though I was aiming for gnosis, and studying and practicing as hard as I could, there was a giant puzzle piece missing that affected by ability to deeply understand. This affected all these encounters with the world.

My relationship with Knowledge was limited by this. And that is okay. As I said, Knowledge changes and deepens over time, as long as outside input is welcomed and embraced.

In my quest to know myself, I have come to know the world. In my quest to know the world, I have come to know myself.

That cycle continues as I age, and I feel gratitude for that.

KNOWLEDGE AND TIME

The young know things the old do not. The old know things the young do not.

Knowledge is not a linear accrual of information. Knowledge rises and falls like air currents, and we rise and descend along with it. Our intellect and consciousness are both flexible, or they were when we were children.

As adults, our intellect and consciousness remain only as flexible as we are willing to remain open. A supple mind requires stretching and lifting, just like our other muscles. And, just as our arms and legs can grow stiff and weak as we age, so can our mind.

But inflexibility is not the hallmark of the old. That can actually happen at any age. We sometimes associate inflexibility with aging simply because of force of habit. But the young can often view the world more through a starkly divided lens. There is black or white, without a rainbow in between.

Some of us spend our teenage and young adult years insisting on binary thinking, based upon the knowledge that we have. Others of us grow into this rigidity, whether because we fear upheaval, or because we've gotten used to our worldview and see no need to change.

In this way, the passage of time affects our relationship to knowledge differently. So, we must return to the dictum "know thyself" and examine what our current patterns are, and why.

Regardless of how much time we have spent on this planet, a radical shift in perspective can be a challenge for any of us.

How often have we been unready for a truth or a different perspective? What knowledge have we rejected because it did not fit our confirmation bias? Our upbringing, beliefs, and worldview all influence our response to new ideas. So do the people we surround ourselves with, the books we read, the music we listen to, and the news we have access to.

Context and time work together to help us craft and assimilate knowledge.

Practice:

What age are you? How flexible is your thinking? How flexible was it five years ago? Or, if you are older, twenty or forty years ago?

In what ways—large or small—are you willing to expand your thinking? Will you listen to a new podcast? Read a book or 'zine written by someone from a different culture, background, or age than you?

Will you take on a meditation practice? Work with a personal trainer on strength and flexibility?

All of these, believe it or not, can increase our data points, offer more information, and help us assimilate knowledge in new ways.

RECLAIMING KNOWLEDGE AND LEARNING

Take a breath. Feel all the facets of yourself. Mind. Spirit. Emotions. Body. Personality. Skills. Talents. Practice.

Now think of your relationships with the world around you. Your education. Interests. Teachers. Students. Mentors. Individuals. Groups. Institutions.

What limitations have been imposed upon your knowledge? Have you been forced into certain courses of study? What have you learned, regardless? Or what have you not learned?

Speaking of learning: How do you learn best? There are so many ways to learn. Doing. Watching. Listening. Reading. Some combination of the above. Some of us learn quickly. Others need time to ruminate. For most of us, this will vary, situation to situation and subject to subject.

What if your brain works differently than most of those around you? I know mine does. What happens to learning then? Do you have space in your life to assimilate knowledge, or does the impatience or misunderstanding of others impede this?

How have you learned to learn?

I had to train myself to learn as an adult, because as a child, not knowing something got me punished. Therefore, I gravitated only toward the things I was more naturally good at. This worked to my detriment, until I painstakingly learned how to learn.

Now I love learning, at least in general! I also have a much better sense of what it is worth my time to try to learn, and what I'm better off asking for help with, from the start, even down to asking or paying someone else to do the work for me.

To claim our ability to learn is to claim our knowledge. Learning changes ourselves, enabling us to process and digest both data and information, until finally, we can say, "I know."

How powerful is that?

PRACTICE:

Read this through as many times as you need to before

engaging with this exercise. As always, if you find yourself constricting, slow down your breathing. Exhale on a sigh, and imagine you can relax your edges.

Approach this practice of calling back knowledge the same way I hope we can all approach learning something new: take a breath and allow yourself to try.

Breathe in life force. Pause. Exhale connection with all living beings. Pause.

Breathe in life force. Pause. Exhale connection with all living beings. Pause.

Breathe in life force. Pause. Exhale connection with all living beings. Pause...

Think of your relationship to your self. Think of all your experiences, whether they feel good, bad, or neutral. Think of what has damaged you and lifted you up. How has all of this affected what and how you learn? How has this informed what you know?

Have you been punished for not knowing? Have you been expected to know everything? Have you been told you know nothing, or are stupid, dense, or out of touch? Have you been praised for your knowledge? Have you faced high expectations because of what you know?

When has someone else's knowledge—or ignorance—been used against you? When has the pressure to learn or not learn, know or not know, caused you to diminish or strike out?

On each inhalation, begin the process of calling Knowledge back.

Call Knowledge back from everyone who mistreated you out of ignorance.

Call Knowledge back from whomever told you that you that you could not or should not learn.

Call Knowledge back from any person or institution who told you certain people have a lesser intellect.

Call Knowledge back from your fear of being wrong.

Call Knowledge back from institutions that claim to be the only pathway toward gaining knowledge.

Call Knowledge back from fear.

Call Knowledge back from the harsh dismissal of your experience.

Call Knowledge back from every time you allowed yourself to feel puffed up by what you know.

Call Knowledge back from each time you felt ashamed of the struggle to learn.

Call Knowledge back.

Breathe it in.

Expand around it.

Say, "I claim my own awareness and experience. I claim the information from my mind and from my senses. I claim my ability to learn, to grow, and to understand. I claim my relationship to Knowledge itself."

Fill up with life. Fill up with the energy of Knowledge, whatever that looks or feels like to you.

Keep breathing.

Keep claiming your connection to the power of Knowledge.

LIBERTY

The pattern of the pentacle continues, flowing across our hearts from Knowledge, illuminating a point in our right hand.

Liberty, rooted in earth, stems from the point of Power. In fact, in Victor Anderson's first formulation of the Pearl Pentacle, this point was called Power. That was how I first learned the point, early in my magical training. It was power raised to a higher octave. Connective, shared power, rather than personal power.

A power whose whole becomes more than the simple sum of its parts.

In my personal estimation, we could even include spiritual power into this formulation, if one wished. I only came to this awareness a decade or so later, after more deeply integrating the reality that spiritual power connects us with beings in all the realms seen and unseen.

When I later studied with him, Victor called this point

Liberty. That made a deep, visceral sense to me, tolling like a gong inside my body. Why? Claiming our inner power leads to inner freedom. Practicing power with others leads to collective liberation.

To quote the great James Baldwin, "Freedom belongs to those who take it."

There is no liberty without power. Power-over naturally suppresses all attempts at collective power, curtailing freedom at every turn. Power-over seeks to impose constraint and limit autonomy.

As liberty is a lack of constraint, and freedom requires autonomy, both facets of this point exist in direct challenge to systems of oppression and control.

We liberate each other and liberate ourselves.

I like to think of the ways power and liberty are connected to the earth. To our bodies. To work. To the basic, material stuff of life. Neither power nor liberty are simple concepts, though sometimes society likes to relegate them to the realm of ideas. They are not.

If power is our ability to do, liberty is our ability to be. To be ourselves. To be with each other. To live our lives as freely as the birds flying through the sky.

One thing I love about birds is that most of them are collective creatures. Watching the crows in my urban neighborhood, I can see the ways they survive because of how well the whole is doing. Uncaged, they help raise each other's hatchlings. They have meetings in the trees each evening, calling out to one another as they wing their way toward their friends.

Yes, I have seen crows squabbling. I've seen them steal from each other. But there seems to be a truth that the crows know, especially as they roost together when winter's cold arrives: without each other, they will die.

Without each other, we will die. So, hoarding power does not make sense. Working on only our inner freedom makes no sense.

Power raised to liberty brings us into the reality of our lives, over and over again: we humans fail when we think we don't rely on one another. We humans fail when we have the hubris to act as if we do not belong to this earth, this cosmos, and all the cycles therein.

Liberty, for me, is not an ideal. Liberty arises from the soil beneath the concrete I walk upon. Liberty is never for me alone. My power and ability to do may help my own life, but the reality is, I have no power on my own. I never have, and never will.

Liberation is a collective activity. The more we cultivate our power within and share our power with others, the more quickly liberation arrives.

The energy of liberty is the energy of our freedom, together. Otherwise, what is our power for?

WHAT IS LIBERTY?

Liberty is the flock of crows, winging through the autumn sky.

Liberty is our voices, raised together in song.

Liberty is in our bodies as we dance in the nightclub or around the fire.

Liberty is the breaking of chains.

Liberty is the unlocking of cages.

Liberty is the insistence upon our personal and collective autonomy.

Liberty claims our sense of power.

Liberty frees us to be as we are.

Liberty insists we all are not the same.

To invoke liberty is to invoke justice. Justice is rooted in the confluence of love and power. Liberty is the public expression of all that I hold dear, and all that fascists and oppressors fear.

Liberty is never given by an outside force. Instead, liberty arises from collective will, creativity, and power. For what is liberty, if not a life in tune with other lives? A liberated life is a life lived in greater harmony with the natural world. Collective liberation is based in the recognition that all of us are nature, too. Each of us is one sacred part of the sacred whole.

Liberation—like power, and like the cycles of the earth, moon, sun, and stars—is also a process. Liberty is not a one-and-done activity. Liberation requires a cascade of choices that continuously bring us back to our values, to our collective power, and to our collective creativity and will.

To live in liberty is to live as fully connected as we possibly can.

And over time? That ability expands and contracts as we shift through phases of love and fear.

Every time we choose to not be forced into patterns of fear, liberty rises.

And we reach out a hand, and help each other once again.

PRACTICE:

Let's begin with a personal assessment of our current relationship to the energy of liberty.

Where do you feel liberty or constriction—lack of freedom—in your body?

Where do you feel liberty or constriction in your spiritual life?

In your emotional life?

At work?

At home?

In your communities?

Where might you call back your power?

Can you stretch, and relax—in body, mind, and spirit—allowing the possibility for greater freedom to enter?

LIBERTY AND CONTROL

When we examine systems of power in the overculture, we can clearly see the effects on liberty.

Shared power and liberation take attention and effort. Think of worker-owned collectives. Parents co-ops. Mutual aid groups. All of these require a lot more time and thought than getting a paycheck from a big company, paying someone to care for the children, or outsourcing community help to government.

Note: I am not saying there is anything wrong with working for someone else or paying a babysitter. Not at all. I'm simply trying to highlight how power works in our societies and how that affects both personal and collective liberation.

Freedom requires effort. Why? Because it requires power

and will. Power is our ability to do. Will is intention in action. In the process of reclaiming our power, we take on more responsibility. That may not feel like freedom, but it actually is.

And here, I'll quote rocket scientist and magician Jack Parsons: "Freedom is a two-edged sword of which one edge is liberty and the other responsibility, on which both edges are exceedingly sharp…"

Decades ago, someone at a workshop I was teaching wanted to talk to me about their spiritual life. We went for a short walk. They said they saw something in me that they wanted for themselves. After I listened for a while, I began to talk with them about structure, commitment, and daily spiritual practice.

They shook their head and said, "I don't want to do that! I want to be *free*!"

I'm don't recall exactly what I replied, but I do remember thinking, "If you want what you say you do, you're never going to get it in this way." Nor would they ever really be free.

Remember: freedom is grounded in earth, and that includes structures of support. Structures of support do not just appear; they must be built. That takes power, the ability to do. Our ability to be is based on that. We can't jump the line, bypassing power, and claim liberty.

I'll offer another example: the anarchists I know and have organized with are fully committed to structures of shared power. This means they show up and work. They attend meetings. They work at every level of community health and well-being. Any political activist truly dedicated to community liberation always works at it, because they know power doesn't arise on its own.

PART II: THE IRON AND PEARL PENTACLES

They also know that if they don't put in the work, the systems of power-over and oppression win.

Systems of control take away choices. Relying on outside structures may seem easier at first—comforting, even—but these structures end up stealing both power and liberty from us, leaving us bereft and unable to live our best lives.

All I have to do is look at the massive prison industrial complex in the United States to see what happens when structures of power-over take control and steal our community autonomy and our joy.

Liberation looks like using power to invest in each other's education, caring for children, making sure people are housed and fed. When all of that happens, guess what? Crime rates drop because people have more personal power. They feel a greater sense of freedom and autonomy. They can see the ways in which healthy community supports every member therein.

The more we give away our power and think that our personal freedom is not deeply connected to everyone and everything else? The more our chances at true liberty are stolen from us.

Once this happens, we have to start over, building once again from the ground up. Learning what our own power is. Remembering how to share power. Remembering what it feels like to laugh with our friends. Feeling the satisfaction of a building a community garden, sharing food, or trading skills.

So, we have choices:

We can confront systems of oppressive power.

We can build systems of shared power and mutual aid.

We can help one another toward true freedom.

Or...we can continue to let our choices be made for us, and

think the remaining scraps we are allowed are the things that make us free.

PRACTICE:

What might healthy community look and feel like to you? What skills do you bring? Really think about it. Don't discount the power you have.

What do you bring to the table of liberty?

What are you willing to do to help build that table?

CULTIVATING LIBERTY

Take a breath. Think back on the times in your life when you felt most free.

Some of us zero in on some life phases or moments instantly. Others may have trouble finding any examples at all. That is okay. It is all information.

How do you feel when you think back on these times of relative freedom? Or how do you feel at the lack of any memories like these?

If you have memories of a feeling of freedom, what was it that made you feel so free? Was it a lack of worry? A lack of self-consciousness? Was it support from family or friends? Was it is an innate sense of your own power and worth? A connection to a place?

If you don't have these memories, can you sense in your body what it might be like to feel free?

Now think of your relationships with the world around you. How much liberation exists in your varied communities?

PART II: THE IRON AND PEARL PENTACLES

What limitations have been imposed upon you, your family, or your friends? Do these limits feel useful or oppressive?

What are the limitations imposed by your spiritual or religious groups? Are these codes of conduct in the best interests of all the members? Are they designed to help keep the most vulnerable safe and feeling welcomed? Or are these rules designed to control?

Not all limits are bad. It requires discernment to assess which support community health and which fracture or limit well-being.

I worked in a soup kitchen in San Francisco for decades. Our code of conduct was simple: No drugs or alcohol use on site. No fighting. No stealing. Treat each other with respect.

Those rules were about community health and well-being, not limitation. Yes, including the *no drugs on site* rule. Some people showed up drunk or high and were welcomed to the courtyard garden. Others showed up sober, and were welcomed, too. Some were en route to work and stopped to get what might have been their one meal of the day.

Did I have to break up fights? Yes. Did I have to kick people out for the day, or a week, or a month, or six months? Sometimes.

The thing was, everyone knew quite clearly what the rules were and why they were in place. Everyone knew it was in their best interests to keep the peace, as well as they were able to. As a result, for many guests, it was the one place they could find rest.

The most important component of these guidelines, though? We were all in relationship with one another. No one was a stranger. We formed our strange, ad hoc community, day after day, year after year.

The guidelines offered a small amount of freedom to us all: a safe place to be, with food, showers, and roses to sit among, and a dining room filled with plants and conversation.

Liberty doesn't have to be perfect. It doesn't even have to be large. Sometimes, liberty is built in the small pockets we create. Together.

If we build enough of these pockets of liberation, and string them together? Think of the world we could create.

PRACTICE:

Read this through as many times as you need to before engaging with this exercise. As always, if you find yourself constricting, slow down your breathing. Exhale on a sigh, and imagine you can relax your edges.

Approach this practice of calling back liberty the same way I hope we can all approach learning something new: take a breath and allow yourself to try.

Breathe in life force. Pause. Exhale connection with all living beings. Pause.

Breathe in life force. Pause. Exhale connection with all living beings. Pause.

Breathe in life force. Pause. Exhale connection with all living beings. Pause...

Think of your relationship to your power. Think of all your experiences with people, situations, or institutions. Think of what has strengthened you or caused you to stumble. How has all of this affected your sense of autonomy? How has this helped or hindered your ability to feel free?

How freely could you move through the world as a child? A teen? An adult? How much oppression or constriction has been forced upon you or your communities? When have others encouraged you to dig into your power? When has liberation been encouraged?

When has power-over been used against you or your loved ones? When have you been chastised for expressions of personal or collective freedom? When has group autonomy been threatened, or personal autonomy been belittled or scorned?

On each inhalation, begin the process of calling Liberty back.

Call the energy of Liberty back from every institution that wants you to live under its control.

Call Liberty back from systems of punishment and the people who help run them.

Call Liberty back from whomever told you that you have no power and, therefore, do not deserve freedom.

Call Liberty back from false ideals of freedom.

Call Liberty back from freedom for some, but not for all.

Call Liberty back from your own fear.

Call Liberty back from feeling you have to do this work alone.

Call Liberty back from the sort of constriction that seeks to keep you small.

Call Liberty back.

Breathe it in.

Expand around it.

Say, "I claim my own power and autonomy. I claim the right to free expression. I claim freedom for my communities, my comrades, my family, and my friends. I claim my ability to grow and change, rooted on this earth. I claim my relationship to Liberty itself."

Fill up with life. Fill up with the energy of Liberty, whatever that looks or feels like to you.

Keep breathing.

Keep claiming your connection to the power of Liberty.

WISDOM

The pattern of the Pearl Pentacle is almost set, as the energy moves from our right hand down into our left foot, lighting up Wisdom.

Wisdom flows like water around rocks, carving out spaces. Wisdom, like water, soothes hurts and cools burns. Wisdom, like water, shapes and forms vast landscapes over time.

Wisdom, based in the energy of Passion, changes us from within.

To be passionate about something is to be fully engaged. How often do we allow this? How often are we supported in our passions? I ask these questions because, without the full engagement of passion, wisdom has no chance to live.

Think of the way knowledge arises from our connection to self. The same is true for passion and wisdom.

If I am not fully engaged with a process—be that my relationships, a craft, spiritual practice, or life itself—I cannot expect to accrue wisdom. I'm thinking back on the formation of the physical pearl, and how the nacre slowly coats the grit within the mollusk, forming something new from it.

Without engagement, the rough edges of my learning are never polished into a smooth form. Without passion, my relationship with life—or craft, or practice, or anything else—does not last long enough for wisdom to emerge.

We cannot force wisdom. Contrary to popular sentiment, wisdom does not naturally arise from age. Time is a factor in wisdom's power, of course, but not the only factor. Think of all the older humans on this planet who are not wise at all. They have steeped themselves in ignorance or apathy, and, for some of them, their passions are rooted only in hatred or disconnection. Apathy and hatred do not foster wisdom, no matter how much time we give them.

To become wise is to live as fully as we can. The more we retreat from life, the more our wisdom dims.

Acupuncturist and author Bonnie Koenig reminded me that the water element is also associated with wisdom in Chinese medicine. She says, "When water works well, there is wisdom. When the energy of water is lacking, then there is fear."

Bruce Lee enjoined us to be like water. To be like water is to invoke flexibility, not fear. After long practice, our actions become effortless, because we have fully entered the flow, finding a way around or through.

WHAT IS WISDOM?

Wisdom is knowing when to speak.
    Wisdom is knowing when to keep silent.
    Wisdom is sensing when to act, and when to remain still.

Wisdom answers the questions three layers down from the surface.

Wisdom understands what we have not even been taught.

How does it do that? Wisdom is the accrual of deep comprehension, in body, emotion, spirit, and mind. This fully integrated comprehension comes from years—often decades—of practice and study. Wisdom comes from deeply, passionately engaging with all facets of ourselves and the world.

Wisdom seeps from our pores like water seeps through sand and pebbles. Wisdom claims nothing, because it is simply part of what is.

Wisdom allows the long-term spiritual practitioner to say, "I am," as a complete sentence.

Wisdom infuses mastery of all sorts. But this is not a static mastery. True mastery is generous, and shares itself with the world.

True wisdom, as I've said, comes from full and passionate engagement, over time.

We sometimes like to speak of the "wise child," but, though a child may have insight, and tell truths that adults would often rather avoid, a child is not truly wise. They seem so, because they carry that forthright energy of the oldest sage. There is an innocence to both ends of this spectrum. But the child has not integrated the lessons of life. It has not studied. It has not stumbled and gotten up again.

Esoteric philosopher Ken Wilbur speaks of pre-rational states of consciousness and how they can look and feel similar to what he calls "trans-rational" states. There is the difference between approaching the ocean, catching our first glimpses of the powerful vastness of it, and looking back on a stretch of ocean already crossed.

The emotions, and how we speak of these experiences, may seem similar on the surface, but only one who has battled open water becomes changed in the ways that wisdom requires.

Wisdom arises from passion and experience, and the joyful, hard-won integration that only comes from both.

PRACTICE:

Gaze into a cup or dish of water, or a river, stream, pond, or ocean if you have access to wild water nearby.

Slow your breathing down. In what ways is your life like this water? What lessons might it teach you?

Now, wherever you are—or after you get home—imagine you can float on top of a calm body of water. Feel yourself cradled and caressed by it. Relax.

Let well-being fill you. Feel all the ways—even deeply buried—in which you are already wise.

If you cannot access that sense of wisdom, that is okay. Keep breathing and relaxing.

Let water teach you what it will.

COMMUNAL WISDOM

There is a special alchemy that happens when a group of people work together over many years. There's a symbiosis that happens, and a group mind that forms, becoming more than its parts.

The group has to allow each member to bring their talents

and knowledge to the table in order for this to happen. If there are too many power struggles, or too much jockeying for position, the group never deepens, and wisdom never arises.

If each person is allowed to express their passion for the work at hand—regardless of what it is—their wisdom grows. When the group makes space for this wisdom, the wisdom of the group mind increases, making the longevity of the group a thing of value, a gift to the larger communities the group may touch or be part of.

This is true in magical or spiritual groups, in activist and social justice spaces, in families, in arts collectives, or in the rarest of work environments.

I'm fortunate to have witnessed this in action a few times in my life. One is with a group of magical people I've steadily worked with for two decades. We are a solid, diverse group, each with different talents. We've had conflicts over the years, but have managed to ride through them. Occasionally, we bring new people into the fold, giving them time to integrate with our group mind, and sharing our collective wisdom.

Are there ways in which we could be healthier? Sure. But that doesn't take away the fact that our longevity is part of our strength. We are committed to each other and the work, even as personality conflicts arise.

We are then able to share our collective wisdom with others, and do longer term work, too.

I've also seen this with some justice groups. I was privileged to work with some activists in Oakland, California, who had been at it for as long as I'd been alive. They were instrumental in seeding and nurturing groups.

I worked with others who had taken on the mantle of

groups that had been active locally decades before, carrying forward a chain of collective wisdom that would have otherwise died.

This is powerful. I've also felt the absence of that in justice groups. Where each group had to reinvent the wheel every two, or five, or ten years. None of the knowledge of the earlier groups remained, let alone any wisdom. Why? The earlier people in leadership got chewed up or burned out. There was no one left to carry on.

Sometimes this sort of burnout feels inevitable, but it is not.

The joy of collective wisdom is that it makes space to back off when needed, to rest when needed, and to pass the work along. Just as water moves, so wisdom does, too. Water ebbs and flows. When it becomes stagnant, things rot.

Passionate engagement is the opposite of stagnation. Passionate engagement allows us to grow and deepen, to expand and flow.

PRACTICE:

What examples do you have of collective wisdom? What inspiration can you take from these examples?

If you don't have any examples, talk to your friends about this topic. Do they have examples?

And, what is one way you might help build collective wisdom over time?

WHEN WISDOM FAILS

I touched on it in the previous section, but want to revisit institutional failure here.

There are many illustrations of what happens when wisdom fails. This most often occurs in two ways. One is the single point of failure problem. When too much skill, knowledge, and wisdom are tied up in one person, instead of shared among many, what happens when that person gets sick, moves away, retires, or simply quits?

The other failure is all too common: people in leadership assume that institutional knowledge is baked in, and that the wisdom accrued by the engagement of individuals is not important to the whole. They see how things are functioning, but not why. They assume everything will continue to run smoothly, even if they fire or relocate some people on the team.

This is not true. Collective wisdom resides in the body of the group, helping the group to function, it is true. However, this is dependent on the engaged experience of many people working together. We can't just slot in someone new and expect the group wisdom to not be changed. Sometimes this change is a good, vital, necessary thing, but other times? It is disastrous.

Another way communal wisdom fails is a lack of recognition that we aren't simply passing along skills and knowledge. That the withdrawal of wisdom matters.

One example is a ritual planning group I was part of. A small group of us had been running rituals for years, and were getting tired. We did the right thing. We brought new people in, included them in the planning process. They took on ritual roles with our support. We trained them for a couple of years, if I recall correctly.

Then, it was time for the earlier members to go on to do other things. The ritual planning group floundered and failed.

What had happened? First, we didn't realize the new people must not have learned the same way we did. Our second mistake was not realizing we had wisdom, not just skills and knowledge. We'd engaged, passionately serving community for a decade. The removal of that wisdom left a void.

Part of wisdom is understanding how it operates in our lives and connects with the lives of others.

Sometimes the withdrawal or collapse of collective wisdom feels like a terrible end. Other times? It is okay when wisdom fails. Sometimes groups run their course and must be allowed to dissolve. It is our personalities that want them to continue forever.

There is no wrong or right in this discussion. There are only strategies to build and strategies to help us let go. The trick is being wise and experienced enough to know the difference.

If a group's survival hinges on one or two people's presence, that group is likely not meant to survive. And that's okay.

PRACTICE:

Imagine you hold a shining thing in your heart and hands. This might be a jewel, a bird, the refrain of a song, or a sense of well-being. Whatever this is, honor it. Surround it with love. Thank this shining thing.

Then let it go.

Feel the space it leaves. It is okay if you feel fear or sadness around this.

Take a breath. Now allow yourself to feel the possibility left by the absence.

Feel your own wisdom slowly seep into the space of possibility, and know that you, too, now have a chance to bring your passion to something new. Something you may not be able to see or feel yet.

But that something is on its way.

CULTIVATING WISDOM

Drop into yourself. Notice your body, emotions, and the space around you.

Do you feel any passion in your life right now? If not, that is where you will begin. Return to the Iron Pentacle and do some passion work. See what happens.

That said, I also challenge each of us to find something with even the smallest drop of passion in it. Perhaps it is caring for a friend, parent, or child. Perhaps it is your commitment to a social cause: protecting the forest, or queer youth, or immigrants, or something else. Perhaps it is your current favorite song, or something else that engages your emotions. Perhaps it is a project you've been working on that you just keep trying to figure out.

Passion does not always need to feel huge or grandiose. Passion can be as small as a whisper that won't be silenced. Passion can be a single drop or a whole ocean.

Sometimes, in order to notice passion, we must allow ourselves to honor the things we are already connected to.

So, with that in mind, let us change the question: Where in your life do you feel wise? What wisdom have your experiences instilled in you? In what ways have you engaged with practice, dedicated yourself to something, and done it long enough that knowledge has deepened into wisdom?

We all have the potential for wisdom inside us, but we have to allow it first. We begin to chip away at the defenses of self-abnegation, discounting our worth, or puffing ourselves up to mask our insecurities.

To become wise is to offer ourselves grace.

To become wise is to keep showing up for what feels important, even when we are filled with doubt.

To become wise is to enter into the flow of time.

Practice:

Read this through as many times as you need to. As always, if you find yourself constricting, slow down your breathing. Exhale on a sigh, and imagine you can relax your edges.

We call back wisdom by opening space for it.

Breathe in life force. Pause. Exhale connection with all living beings. Pause.

Breathe in life force. Pause. Exhale connection with all living beings. Pause.

Breathe in life force. Pause. Exhale connection with all living beings. Pause...

Think of your relationship to your passion.

In which areas of your life do you feel you fully engaged? Where do your passions reside?

In what ways do you feel a sense of mastery?

Do you have moments where wisdom flows through you? What does that feel like?

Think of all your experiences with people, situations, or institutions. When has your passion been undervalued? When has your hard-won wisdom been dismissed?

How often were you allowed to explore your interests as a child? A teen? An adult? Were you teased for being passionately engaged with something? Or were you forced to work too hard on an interest, causing your passion to diminish?

When were your passions encouraged?

When was your wisdom honored?

How often have you honored your own wisdom?

When has your experience been undervalued? When has it been sought out, as a gift?

When have you doubted or suppressed your inner voice?

On each inhalation, begin the process of calling Wisdom back.

Call the energy of Wisdom back from every institution that wants to belittle your insight.

Call Wisdom back from people who think their knowledge is more important than your lived experience.

Call Wisdom back from situations who tried to say you were delusional or out of touch.

Call Wisdom back from manipulative so-called gurus.

Call Wisdom back from so-called influencers or experts.

Call Wisdom back from your own diminishment.

Call Wisdom back from feeling if others are wise, you can't be, too.

Call Wisdom back from fearing the passion that gets you in the flow.

Call Wisdom back.

Breathe it in.

Expand around it.

Say, "I claim my own lived experience. I claim my inner voice and intuition. I claim my passions. I claim the right to celebrate my friend's experience and passions, too. I claim the deep tugging inside me that points me in the right direction. I claim the buried jewels inside my soul. I claim my relationship to Wisdom itself."

Fill up with life. Fill up with the energy of Wisdom, whatever that looks or feels like to you.

Keep breathing.

Keep claiming your connection to the power of Wisdom.

THE CYCLE CONTINUES

And so, Wisdom cycles back to Love, and then a sunwise circle moves from Love, to Knowledge, to Wisdom, to Law, to Liberty, to Love. This sunwise circle balances these energies within us, and in the world.

Let the lines connecting the points in the star shape help cleanse and activate the energies within us. Allow the sunwise circle to seal those qualities within us, and then, as the circle turns, feel Love, Knowledge, Wisdom, Law, and Love radiate out into the world.

That sunwise circle brings healing to us and all our relationships. The sunwise circle has the energetic capacity to enliven and bring greater balance and healing to the planet and the cosmos.

When life force feeds love, we can connect in healthier ways. When our love connects with knowledge, our understanding deepens. Engaged with knowledge, we invoke wisdom over time. From this place of wisdom, we invoke the clarity of natural law, of balance, and true justice. This clarity of law brings us to liberty, to freedom for all. This brings us further into relationship with community, to the elements, and then reaching back to the flow of life force, we return again to a state of love.

SUNWISE AND ANTI-SUNWISE

Anyone who is paying attention sees what happens when the points of the Pearl Pentacle are manipulated and twisted by bad actors in the world, or sometimes even by bad actors in the unseen places, be those larger, institutional patterns that have taken on a life of their own, or beings from other realms.

When love only of those closest to us runs anti-sunwise into liberty only for those we deem useful to us, the powers begin to twist in ugly ways. Laws are built to cage, kill, or exploit those deemed lesser, or simply different. Wisdom that grows from this is not wisdom at all, but conventional opinion that upholds the status quo. This is bolstered by knowledge based on skewed data and information that only confirms our biases. And all of that flows back into a poisonous attitude that is called love in name only.

By working the Pearl Pentacle, whether alone or in community, we invoke the sunwise turn to counter this abomination.

It is up to us to continue the magic and manifest a world where change is for the good of all.

Together.

PART III: AUTONOMY AND WILL

THE PENTACLE OF AUTONOMY

The Pentacle of Autonomy is a tool to help bring our lives into greater integrity. We move further into true adulthood, accepting responsibility, and recognizing the ways in which we can be of service.

When I first developed this pentacle, I called it the Warrior's Pentacle. I used it as a way to help strengthen both will and heart, self and community.

I've since used it to teach leadership, and as a way for us to show up for what we love.

I changed the name to the Pentacle of Autonomy somewhere along the way. The points on this pentacle—Commitment, Honor, Truth, Strength, and Compassion—resonate with and bridge the points on Iron and Pearl and contain echoes of the Elemental Pentacle as well.

THE WARRIOR'S HEART

I have to admit, sometimes it feels hard to engage the warrior's heart, especially when it feels most necessary. Everyone is worn out. Tired. We've had years of conflict, upheaval, and uprisings followed by pandemics and more upheaval, followed by rising authoritarianism and fascism.

This makes it all the more important to engage with the world, calling upon commitment and compassion. We all need to keep finding ways to adjust, rethink, rework, and find a way through. The Pentacle of Autonomy is a tool that can help us with this process.

There will never be a perfect time or place to show up. We will rarely be in the perfect position to help. We won't have our lives perfectly together. So, what do we do? We become willing to take a risk from our imperfectly perfect selves and to find a way to simply act. We become more willing to try.

One thing that helps me is to get increasingly specific about what exactly I am fighting for. I may not always be able to tackle larger things, but can I support one person's efforts? Can I speak out on one injustice? Can I feed one person? Can I organize with my friends around issues affecting our home community? Can we organize with a larger group around the larger issues?

And, in the midst of all of this, can I find one small way to support my own dreams and desires? Can I find ways to keep committing to the dailiness of life, and to my creativity and magic?

When the world feels overwhelming, and we feel too tired to pick up our sword and charge into battle, we can still find a way through. We can still commit.

The Pentacle of Autonomy offers us a path toward action.

We can keep finding ways through, even on days when it may feel impossible.

STRONG WILL, OPEN HEART

What in you wants or is willing to show up for what you love? What are you passionate about? What do you see that is wrong that you wish to help correct? What do you see that is right that you wish to help support? What battles are you willing to commit to?

Why is it important to be a warrior, teacher, parent, healer, artist, or organizer right now? There are myriad things wrong, so we need to pick something and channel our passion there.

Otherwise, the world gets overwhelming and all we want to do is crawl back into bed or numb ourselves.

Feeling constantly overwhelmed, grief-stricken, frustrated, or beaten down by the state of the world does not help the world. Overwhelm does not help us face ourselves and the world with compassion.

I often say, "Do what you can, when you can, where you can." This is an encapsulation of so much of this work with the Pentacle of Autonomy and showing up. The phrase reminds us to assess our current internal state and capacity and bring those to our assessment of what is in front of us, externally.

What is needed? How can I show up? Where is the entry point? What is my strategy? What are my tactics?

Why is it important to you to strengthen your will and open your heart? Why is it important to live with integrity and honor? Why is it important to show up again and again?

EXPLORING THE PENTACLE

This is a pentacle for warriors, parents, healers, teachers, activists, organizers, and creatives.

It begins with Commitment. Commitment is the opening and beginning of everything. Even if all we commit to is study, or curiosity, or showing up for a moment, that is where we start. We begin with commitment and that builds over time as we cycle through the rest of the points.

Commitment moves into Honor. We must honor our commitments and develop integrity and integration. Honor flows into Truth. Truth is not only about telling the truth about ourselves and our lives, it is also a state of embodied alignment.

So, Commitment flows to Honor, flows to Truth. All of that feeds into Strength. It feeds power and integrated will, and all the other things we think of when we mention strength. From a place of strength, we flow into

Compassion. Compassion is an open-hearted state of connection, of curiosity about ourselves, other people, and the situations we find ourselves in together.

So we start with Commitment, and flow through Honor, Truth, Strength, and Compassion. All of that flows back to feed Commitment. We get to choose, again, to recommit, in an even stronger and more clear way. We are able to reassess our commitments. We get a chance to say, "Yes, I commit. Yes, I will honor this commitment. Yes, I am trying to live in truth with this commitment. Yes, I have strength I bring to bear on this commitment. Yes, I have compassion, and I bring that to the work at hand. And yes, I am willing to recommit. Again."

Practice:

Take a breath let these concepts move through you for a moment: Commitment. Honor. Truth. Strength. Compassion. Commitment.

Pick a color that you'd like to work with. For me, I like the clarity of golden yellow.

Imagine Commitment in your head, flowing from Spirit and bridging Sex and Love. Now, allow that energy to move through you toward your left foot.

Arising from Fire, Honor bridges Pride and Law.

The energy flows up through your body into your left hand. Moving from Air, let Truth resonate with Self and Knowledge.

Then, flow across your heart to your right hand. Grounded in Earth, Strength assists Power and Liberty. Flowing down into your left foot, immersed in Water, allow Compassion to link both Passion and Wisdom.

And all of this returns again to Commitment.

You can run this pentacle on its own, without linking it to the others, but I often find working the resonances helpful, too.

COMMITMENT

This pentacle begins and ends with commitment

What does it mean to commit ourselves? It means to show up as fully as we can in the moment. Not half-hearted. Not half-assed. Fully saying, "I am here now, with this task, this ideal, this person…I commit."

I commit to myself. I commit to you. I commit to this project. I commit to my beliefs. I put action behind my belief. It's not just lip service. I'm not just saying something. I'm enacting when I commit.

Commitment requires follow-through; otherwise, it isn't commitment.

So, what are you committing to, today? Take a breath into that.

You're committing to reading this, right now, hoping you might learn something, or it might spark an idea you hadn't considered before. Or it might help you revisit things you've thought about in the past...so, you're committing to that, at the most basic level.

What about family commitments? Commitments to friends? To your art? To justice? What about longer, larger life commitments?

Do you have hopes and dreams? Everyone who has hopes and dreams has to commit to something first, before enacting those hopes and dreams. And again, here we start with the smallest commitment. If I want to write a novel, I don't commit to a novel. Not at first. I first commit to the excitement of the idea. Then I commit to writing that first sentence. And the next. And then I commit to continuity. In order to write a novel, I must have continuous commitments, whether that's every day, or a few times a week. Without continuous commitment, the novel will never get written. There won't be enough sentence strung together to form the story, let alone something I've completed that I can then share with others.

So, my first commitment is: I'm going to sit down and write. Then I'm going to keep writing. Then I'm going to finish and publish. Then I'm going to write the next book, starting again with one idea and that first sentence.

Every time I begin again, I'm stronger and more capable and have a greater ability to follow through on my commitment. So, the energy of commitment builds.

But before I started that, I had to commit to myself in other ways. I had to commit to my health. I have an autoimmune disorder, the aftermath of a brain injury that comes and goes, I'm aging...I need to make sure I get enough rest. I need to go for a daily walk and get other forms of exercise. I need to make sure I'm eating the kinds of food that help me be as effective and healthy as possible. All of this also means I need to listen for the days I just need to rest. All of this is part of my general commitment to health.

I also have commitments to my family. To my spiritual practice. To mutual aid and social justice. But currently, all of my commitments must—by necessity—follow my basic commitment to my physical health.

Commitment becomes a cascade, with each component building upon the next, rippling out into our lives and the lives of others.

Commitment is the small seed we plant—and water and fertilize and tend—that grows and eventually bears fruit. Commitment therefore requires a certain amount of patience.

We have to keep showing up. Commitment requires time.

What are you willing to commit to, even just for today? And what is the larger commitment that might serve?

What is your hope? Your desire? Your dream? Walk that back. What is the first commitment you can start with that will support your hopes, desires, and dreams?

COMMITMENT AND WILL

Work begins with commitment and continues with recommitment. This sometimes requires discipline, which I would like to unhook here from any punitive feelings we may carry about the word.

Until we commit, taking a risk, nothing can begin from our own volition. Things may happen around us, and happen to us, but nothing will happen from a place of our choosing. This is very important to recognize.

To have choice, we cultivate will. Will is built on willingness. We must have a willingness to act or not act. Will is intention in action. Habit-building activities can help strengthen our will. That dreaded word, discipline—which literally means "to take on a teaching"—also bolsters our will.

The stronger our will and willingness, the more profound our ability to choose.

What is your current relationship to discipline, to cultivating habits, or to recommitting to the actions you have set yourself?

It is okay to fall out of practice and need to recommit. It is okay to chafe at discipline or need a break. But if we have made a commitment, there comes a time when we must recognize how important it is to us.

If the thing we've committed to is important, we will make the effort and take the time to follow through. If not, we may need to reassess our commitment. We'll do more work around this during the Honor point.

Practice One:

What are you willing to commit to? What matters to you? What are the first steps necessary to fulfill that commitment?

Set a timer. Write for five minutes and see what comes up. Don't stop—don't pause to ponder or worry—until the time is up. Now, read back what you wrote. Are you, in this moment, able to follow through on this in some small way? What is the next step to engage this commitment more fully?

Write that first step down. Now come up with a plan to follow through on that first step, and write that down.

What two steps might follow that first? Write those down.

What is your strategy to keep this commitment? How will you follow through?

PRACTICE TWO:

Throughout the coming week, notice the ways you may be engaging with or avoiding your commitment, with no judgement. Let this just be information. Maybe you need to rethink your steps, or adjust the commitment itself. You can always start again, using the following questions as your guide:

What do I commit to in the next five minutes?

What will I commit to today?

What will I commit to this week?

It also helps to look at larger patterns around commitment. Do you have trouble following through in general, or is it just for this particular commitment?

Why do you think that is? What might help you?

SCALING OUR COMMITMENTS

Sometimes we think big. That is great. It is good to imagine what is possible and to see the larger picture. It is good to have ambition.

That said, sometimes this makes our commitments feel overwhelming. When we start big, things can feel impossible. We cannot, as individuals, fix the climate crisis. We cannot, as individuals, fix social injustice. We cannot, as individuals, fix everything that's wrong in our birth families or our communities.

So, we need to take a step back and ask what we can commit to that will be of help and service, and will dovetail with the work other activists, healers, teachers, parents, and organizers are doing in the world? How can my offering hook in with what other people offer?

We co-create the cosmos and society. We do not have to do it all on our own.

Figuring out how to plug in can be one of the most useful acts we can do. So, we scale back and find our next step. Not someone else's next step. Building on those next, smaller steps increases our will and ability to act. This all helps us to honor our commitments.

THE JOY OF COMMITMENT

Fostering joy in the face of commitments might be something we need to work on. Cultivating joy in the midst of work is important.

HONOR

We often think of Honor in terms of warriors, and warrior culture, though that is certainly not the only realm in which this word applies. We think of what it means to be honorable.

To be honorable, for me, means to have integrity. This means that enough of myself is integrated that I'm not working at cross purposes with myself. Nor am I making promises I can't keep. So, I'm not working at cross purposes with my family, my project, my community, my friends.

To have honor means I keep my word.

I show up when I say I'm going to.

I do the thing I said I was going to do. Or if I can't, I'm going to clearly tell you why, and find a way to do it in a different fashion, or make it right some other way.

So, honor is the simple task of showing up for our commitments with as much integrity as we can muster. That's the tricky thing.

How often are we making promises because we want to, and they seemed like a good idea, or we feel that people expect them of us, but we can't really follow through?

Maybe we're too frightened to follow through. Maybe we have anxiety about it. Maybe we don't yet have the skills needed to follow through on whatever the particular promise is. Maybe we promised on a "good" day and our health or brain chemistry has been challenging us since.

So, again, backing up: What changes might be required for our lives to form a platform from which we can honor our commitments to ourselves and our communities or our projects? And, what are we willing to show up for?

The willingness to show up, in itself, feeds and bolsters honor and helps our sense of honor to grow. Just as we practice small steps for our commitments, we can practice honor.

Honor is not something we are born with. Honor is something we develop and learn. We can think of Honor like a craft. We show up to learn wood carving, but we don't learn it overnight. We learn wood carving curl by curl, and angle by angle.

What does it mean to you to honor something or somebody?

Another facet of honor is respect. I must respect myself and you, and I must respect the relationship between us. It is the same with a task. I must respect myself, the task, and the relationship between myself and task. It is the same with community, with social justice, with organizing, fighting for what we believe in.

To honor something is to be willing to fight for it. Sometimes fighting for something is as simple as saying, "I show up.

I follow through. I bring as much of myself to this as I can because I have integrity."

When we have integrity, our hearts, will, and minds all work in concert. Sometimes the mind thinks something is a great idea. That's easy. I have thousands of great ideas, more than I can ever hope to put into practice or bring to fruition. But when there is a concept that I can marry with my heart and my will, then I can honor that impulse. I can make a commitment and show up. I have integrity in that moment, and I can sense it. My parts are working together, like horses in harness pulling the chariot or the wagon.

So, honor, like commitment, is something we can break down into smaller steps. We can work with and develop honor.

We can learn to trust ourselves and trust the process. We can take a breath and deepen our commitment to becoming more honorable people.

We can show up for what we want and believe.\

INTEGRITY

In the world, we see how lack of integrity causes harm. It harms whole communities as well as individuals. It hurts the environment. The earth is on fire. There are massive forest fires eating thousands of hectares. There is flooding. Hurricanes and tornadoes where there were not any before. Climate change is increasing at an alarming pace. There are pandemics. War. Genocide. There is war on individuals and whole communities. War on women. Children. Trans and queer people. Black and Indigenous people. The list goes on.

All of this may seem like a tangent from the topic of integrity, but it is not.

If I cannot develop my own integrity and learn to act honorably, how do I expect anyone around me to act honorably? How do I expect honor in my communities?

So, let's bring this conversation back from the global field, and into our local communities. Our friend groups. Our temples, covens, or lodges. All the groups we may be a part of. How much integrity is there? How much honor is there? How often are we working at cross purposes with one another? How often do people not follow through? How much are people undermining the group identity and purpose?

How often am I—are we—doing any of that?

If we want a world filled with honor, we must commit to honor and integrity ourselves.

We have to learn to say: I honor you. I honor our work and practice together.

Integrity—and lack of integrity—has a huge ripple effect on all of our relationships, including global relationships. If a manufacturer had integrity and honor, they would follow that through the entire manufacturing process, including figuring out what happens when their product reaches the end of its life span. Can it be reused? Repurposed? Recycled? Can it disintegrate back into soil without harming the planet?

Another way manufacturers can practice honor is by paying a living wage and providing safe working conditions. They can practice honor by doing their level best to not pollute the air, water, or soil. They cannot strip whole countries of resources while exploiting workers.

All of this is what honor and integrity might look like in manufacturing.

What does honor look like in multinational corporations? Along with all of the above, is what they are mouthing in their advertising campaigns reflected down to the person answering phones or emptying garbage cans?

How are people and the planet being treated? What is being thought of?

And when we once again scale that back to our own commitments, how far along are we imagining or thinking? Can we be more visionary about our own commitments?

We can't get trapped in the large-scale vision, because then nothing will get done. But we can keep it in mind as we figure out our next steps. As we write the next sentence or take the small action. But it is good to periodically expand outward and think: What is the possible outcome of this commitment? How might honor and integrity thread all the way through?

We need to keep in mind the microcosm, macrocosm, and everything in between. We can play in this entire field. Doing this increases our strength and resiliency and our ability to be honorable.

Keeping the large and small in mind increases our ability to think on what honor and integrity actually mean.

HOW DO WE HONOR COMMITMENTS?

We're all different.

We all have different brains and bodies. We have different relationships to support and trauma. We come from different families and cultures.

So, when it comes to honor, how can you honor your commitments? I know what honoring commitment feels and looks like to me, and there are commonalities we can talk about.

But I'd like to get a bit more granular here.

For example:

If you feel you have trouble with follow-through—because of a particular type of neurodivergence, or because of trauma, or chronic illness, or because of different sorts of oppression and injustice—what sorts of commitments can you honor, and how? Pushing through and trying to establish habits the way a bunch of other people establish habits may not work for you. Or it may work for a while and then become a source of frustration.

Do you have trauma that causes any follow-through that is not "perfect" to make you feel like a failure? Can you reframe what honoring that commitment feels and looks like? Can you come at it from a different angle?

Let's practice taking a breath and saying out loud: "I honor myself, and who I am right now. This is the best I can do in this moment in time. And, more importantly, it is what I can do, not what someone else can do, and not what I think I ought to be able to do."

I used to say: We make magic from where we are, not from where we think we should be.

That goes for honor, too. Don't ask how Thorn honors their commitments, or how your best friend does. Inquire how you honor your commitments. And then ask yourself, "What am I willing to fight for?"

And I hope one of the things you're willing to fight for is yourself.

Begin with a commitment to supporting yourself and the way your brain and body functions, from your life in its current state. Then call upon honor from that first commitment. How can you currently best honor yourself? And how does that affect how you honor your relationships with family, community, and this earth?

What are you willing to fight for, and how?

PRACTICE:
Take some time to answer the following questions:
What is one way I will honor myself?
What is one way I will honor others?
What is one way I will honor this earth?
What is one way I will honor my commitment?

HONORABLY LETTING GO

There's another facet of honor and integrity I'd like to examine.

We've talked about honoring self, each other, communities, and commitments. We've pondered how to live with greater integrity and be more honorable as human beings on this planet.

Sometimes, to be honorable, is learning when to let something go. Sometimes we've taken on a commitment that is not right. Not right for us or our skill set, or our passion isn't there... or our circumstances have changed. Sometimes, we must say, "I'm sorry, but I need to honorably let this commitment go."

How often has someone in your community or workplace—or even yourself—taken on a commitment and then stopped showing up? Stopped answering texts or emails? Done a half-assed job with something?

All of these are signs that either the commitment wasn't right for us or the other person, or we weren't able to honor the commitment. As a consequence, the person—perhaps us—begin to act with less and less honor.

We start calling on avoidance, or assigning blame to someone else, saying "It's out of my control…. It's out of my hands…. Oh, if only we could do something…."

We hear those sorts of things in the world at large, all the time, not only closer to home. Politicians and corporate heads who are doing environmental damage, other people in positions of authority or power-over, frequently sidestep responsibility by using these tactics.

We don't want to do this with our own commitments.

So, what do we do? Sometimes, to truly honor a relationship means we must respectfully release that relationship. We need to dissolve the contract. Even the unwritten ones. We make unspoken contracts with ourselves and others all the time. Are we honoring those social contracts?

Sometimes to honor social contracts we must speak them out loud and make them apparent. Doing so helps us make clear decisions about the contracts and commitments we may be entering into in the first place.

Once our commitments are clear, we can figure out whether we can recommit, and figure out the next task, or the next phase needed to honor the commitment. We can figure out the next way to best show up, with integrity.

Making our commitments and contracts clear also enables us to say, "Respectfully, I must release this contract now. I can no longer honor this commitment, and must let it go."

To clearly and cleanly let something go is honorable.

I'm going to repeat that.

To clearly and cleanly let something go is honorable.

Honor does not mean suffering under the weight of something we're ill-suited for, or ill-equipped for. Nor does honor mean clinging to something whose time has passed for us.

To live honorably is to be as clear and clean in our interactions as we can be in the moment.

So, sometimes honor means to let something go.

PRACTICE:

Think of two commitments you currently have. How clear are they? Is it time to figure out the next steps that will help you fully honor those commitments? Or is it time to honorably release them?

HONORING OUR EFFORTS

In doing this work, it is important to honor the fact that we are trying. We are making efforts toward integrity. To honor ourselves. Honor each other. Honor this planet. Our work. Our communities. Our joy.

Honoring is not all about struggle, though it can sometimes feel that way in midst of the daily crush of work, health, family, or community obligations, and all of life's very real difficulties.

By pausing to celebrate all the ways in which we are

showing up for our lives and our interlocking communities, we enable ourselves to continue another day.

Each time we say, "Today, I'm finding a way to choose to honor my commitments," or, "I choose to honor my life," we should acknowledge this.

Let's celebrate our efforts, and our capacity to show up, because life itself, nature itself, is replete with celebration.

Practice:

Celebrate yourself and your efforts in whatever way feels resonant. This could mean going for a walk in a nature preserve, eating a luscious dessert or a perfectly ripe piece of fruit, dancing in the living room, or one hundred other ways.

Honor yourself by honoring your efforts.

TRUTH

Truth vibrates somewhere between air, self, and knowledge.

What does it mean to be true? True to yourself? True to someone or something else?

I like to return to the root of the word, which is less commonly used in recent years, and that is the concept of alignment.

In the section on honor, we talked about integrity, and integrity and alignment work hand in hand. Something that is dis-integrated can never be aligned. A sword is true when it is forged properly and all the elements come together. There is a whole process to making a sword true. It is hammered, and softened, and hammered again, and layered, and shaped, and finally quenched, setting its form. Aligned.

The same goes for a shovel, rake, or hoe. Bicycle or motorcycle forks must be true in order to hold the tire so the rider can steer properly and move forward.

So, the truer we are to ourselves, the more integrity we have. The more aligned we become, the better able we are to live our truth. We are able to tell the truth about our lives and each other. We can better process information about a situation in which there are likely multiple truths, remaining open to these, and accurately assessing what may be the deeper truth.

The greater our alignment, the more able we are to resonate with various truths. Alignment helps us with discernment.

Without integrity and alignment, our discernment is fractured, and so all of our relationships become fractured. It becomes more difficult to show up. There's a lot more unnecessary and unhelpful friction. Sometimes friction or resistance are necessary. But sometimes they get in the way.

Lack of discernment and lack of inner truth makes it easier for stumbling blocks to come our way. Lack of alignment makes it harder to overcome the stumbling blocks, as well. We're just not as clear. We are not as ready or prepared as we would be were we centered in the truth of ourselves.

Honoring our commitments helps us with preparation and integrity, which allow us to come to into a greater state of alignment, or inner truth.

Alignment helps us know ourselves better.

Our aim in all of our practices is to become closer and closer to truth in the moment, and show up for what we believe in and desire. This truth also helps us show up for our relationships and for what we're working toward collectively, in community.

We can also learn how to better tell the truth, and live our truth. In order to do that, we must ourselves become more true. More present. More aligned.

PRACTICE ONE:

Notice your life. In what areas do you feel in alignment? Where do you feel out of alignment? How do both states affect the different facets of your life?

What is your current truth? What is central to you? What feels important?

How honestly are you living your life and your values? How aligned are you with your thoughts and beliefs?

How often do you speak the truth to the deepest parts of yourself?

How often do you speak the truth to your loved ones?

PRACTICE TWO:

If you have a physical cup or blade, get those now. If not, you can imagine them. They are acting as symbols for your will and your heart, married together to support your truth.

Get into an upright posture for sitting meditation. Whether on a cushion or in a chair, make sure your hips are resting higher than your knees. Feel your spine floating up from your pelvis, and your head resting on your spine. Roll one shoulder back. Then the other. Breathe.

Hold or imagine the tools of cup and blade, one in each hand. Feel the way they balance each other: openness and action, listening and moving, the strong boundary that holds water and emotion coupled with the sharp edge that defines space and intention.

Breathe into your belly and listen for your truth. What rises up, to be fueled by will, embraced by compassion, and honed by your intention?

Speak this truth out loud, uncensored. Invite all the parts of you to listen.

SPEAKING TRUTH TO POWER

"Leave safety behind. Put your body on the line. Stand before the people you fear and speak your mind—even if your voice shakes. When you least expect it, someone may actually listen to what you have to say. Well-aimed slingshots can topple giants."

Maggie Kuhn said that, and she would know. Maggie was a warrior. She founded the Gray Panthers to combat ageism in the workplace and to advocate for nursing home reform in the US. She also fought for other human rights, economic justice, and for the rights of the mentally ill and disabled, all while caring for her own disabled mother and brother.

This quote is often distilled down to, *"Speak the truth, even if your voice shakes."* And that's what courage is, isn't it? Courage is showing up even when we feel afraid.

Civil rights activist and gay man Bayard Rustin coined the phrase *"speak truth to power."* To speak truth to power is to challenge the king. It is to face the systems of authority and corruption and say, "We've had enough." Speaking truth to power means is a slingshot that can topple giants.

Anti-lynching activist and newspaper founder and reporter Ida B. Wells said, *"The way to right wrongs is to shine*

PART III: AUTONOMY AND WILL

the light of truth on them." She lived her whole life doing just that.

What gives you courage to speak the truth? What is your slingshot that can topple giants?

Sometimes we don't know until it happens, don't we? We simply galvanize ourselves, center ourselves in our truth the best we can, join some friends and comrades, and send the stone of truth flying through the air.

What matters is that we try. What matters is that we choose, in that moment, to believe in ourselves and our cause.

What matters is, we speak our truth, starting with ourselves, and then sharing that truth with others.

This is vital work, and work we can all engage in, no matter our current conditions and lot in life. Our greatest strength can come from our deepest wounds, or from the things that make us strange in the eyes of others.

Our wounds and strangeness help make up the truth of who we are. I'll offer a few examples below, if you'd like to look into them further, though you may have examples of your own.

Alice Wong's activism arises from and works with her disabilities, helping countless people—disabled or not—to also speak truth to power. Dr. Devon Price tells the truth about autism, planting seeds, and making change. Bayard Rustin's gayness too often shunted him to the background of the civil rights movement, but he managed to turn that to his advantage, and act as a powerful force in the movement, without becoming a public target himself.

There are many ways to live our truth and fight for what we love, even in the face of discouragement, fear, or even shame.

What is one of yours?

And how will you—or do you—find ways to show up, aligned with your own truth? How will you—or do you—speak truth to power?

ASSESSING TRUTH

How do we bring our truth to our commitments?

We start by assessing and gauging our skills, abilities, health, and passion.

We also assess and gauge our level of commitment.

Not every commitment is massive, or a big deal. Some are small, which is great. We just show up, do the thing, drink our water, meditate, get some exercise, answer that phone call or email, write that paragraph.... These are ways we bring truth to our commitments.

Another way we bring truth is to assess and gauge our relationship to the commitment. What is the truth of the relationship? What is the truth of the situation? How much of myself am I willing to bring to bear? So, again, some commitments require a greater measure of truth.

If I have this commitment to supporting my friend who feeds people who live under the bridge every day, I need to know the scope of that commitment. In my own life, it used to be, I'd go out and help physically, in person. In recent years, because of my autoimmune disorder, I don't have as much energy as I used to. So, the other ways I commit are: Organize a sleeping bag drive. Donate books. Give money. Spread the word to other people. Or I might show up once a week or once a month and make sandwiches. I can offer to pick up supplies on my next grocery run.

PART III: AUTONOMY AND WILL

In all these ways, I assess and engage my level of commitment and am telling the truth about my ability and capacity to honor that commitment. I'm not making commitments I can't honor. By making commitments I can honor, through assessing my abilities and resources, I'm bringing greater truth to that commitment.

I'm acting with integrity. This then reflects back, and helps me become more true, aligned, and upright as a human being. This ensures that I'll have greater clarity of truth to bring to my next commitment.

We all start somewhere. This is an ongoing, cyclical process. We are ever in an evolving relationship. Every situation is slightly different. There is no rubber stamp or one-size-fits-all angle to this.

We want to be engaged. That's it. By engaging, we bring greater truth to the relationship, activity, task, and community. Engagement and integrity help us bring more truth to the things we say we believe in and the things we want to fight for.

Without a sense of our inner truth, our confidence erodes, and other people's confidence in us also erodes. Things begin to fall apart, and nothing gets accomplished. Society continues to churn on. People keep getting hurt. The planet keeps getting hurt.

The more we show up in ways large and small, and try to live out truth, the more becomes possible.

Together.

PRACTICE:

Breathe into the energy of Truth. Feel where the seat of this energy is in your body in the moment. Tap into that. Take three long, slow breaths. Feel your core truth. Feel what is at the heart of your life and commitments. What is core to you? How can you be true to that?

Then, say these words out loud: "I am upright and true. I bring my best, most aligned self to the moment. I enact the world I want to help create."

LIVING IN TRUTH

How do we live our truth?

We learn to live more honorably, with greater integrity, and in a state of greater alignment.

It's helpful to examine the ways in which we are not living in integrity in order to get closer to doing so. For some of us, this may feel like a large project of self-examination, or a life overhaul. For others of us, this means making small adjustments, or examining parts of our lives that we often set to the side. Looking at habits of practice or mind. Attitudes. Speech.

If I say, "I am willing to fight for this cause," but all I do is talk about it with my friends, never taking action, I'm not willing to fight for that cause.

This means I either need to stop saying I'll fight for the cause, or work on developing a stronger will and more open heart.

Without the literal will to follow through, I have not claimed my agency. And without that, I'm never going to live in my truth.

So, for some of us, this examination means we need to back up to will development. Building that muscle that is linked to

PART III: AUTONOMY AND WILL

personal power, agency, autonomy, and our ability—and willingness—to do. To do this is simple, but takes another round of commitment, which can feel hard. We have to show up when we say we'll do something and train all of our parts to not return to the inertia of a body at rest.

Sometimes I call this process "resetting my inertia." I want to enter into a state of inertia that is a body in motion.

Sometimes, when trust is broken—and we've all been in situations like this—we need to go back to basics. We must return to the simplest acts of showing up. We do this both to increase our will and to prove to ourselves and others in our communities that yes, this time we will make good on our word.

How do we practice? That's what is both simple and sometimes hard.

To practice: I'll get up each morning and do ten minutes of stretching. Then, no matter how much I may not want to, I lie out a mat and stretch. Or, if I say I'll write for thirty minutes a day, I set a timer and write. Or I tell a friend I'll help them with a project, and then, instead of making excuses when the day comes, I take a breath, and I help my friend.

This proves to ourselves and the people around us that we are trustworthy. The more we practice, the more our integrity shines through. The more aligned and true we become.

We live our truth by examining our truth. We live our truth, not just by thinking about it, by strengthening our ability to do.

The thing that has helped me the most with Will development is daily spiritual practice. For years, I sat in meditation even when it felt excruciating. I observed all the parts of self that squirmed and fought, and finally settled down.

Sitting in an aligned posture, breathing, makes me less reactive and better able to be proactive. Otherwise, I can be buffeted about by every stray thought or emotion. Or I'm following this new shiny idea—and I have many—instead of returning to the idea I committed to last month or last year.

If I'm always in "ooh, shiny" mode, I'm not living my truth. That shiny mode is a fun way to try out new ideas. It is good to fantasize and dream! That said, living in truth is saying "Yes, I made this commitment and am following through. I'm supporting myself in all the different ways I know how, to strengthen myself in order to do this."

To live our truth, we have to comprehend who we are. At least a little bit. And that is where we start.

Then we say, "Yes. I want this. And I will do this."

Even though it feels hard, bewildering, tedious, or boring, we continue to say, "Yes."

And we will be challenged by this word "yes" at every phase of our lives. We will also be challenged by learning when to say "no." To set a boundary, so we can better keep the commitments closest to our hearts.

No one ever successfully gets through a higher degree in education, or a new project, or starts a new business, or raises children, or forms community without this sense of truth and commitment.

How often have you experienced people not showing up for children? How often have you seen people making and breaking promises? If we experienced this from the adults in our lives when we were young, we internalized this. If you had this done to you repeatedly as a child or young person, it may be hard to think you can live in a state of greater truth and integrity. You did not have that modeled for you.

But, I insist that we can learn to model this for ourselves and for each other. We can show up today.

PRACTICE:

Examine your life, thoughts, and behaviors. Where do you need more practice in showing up to live your truth? How can you strengthen your will?

Now, sit or stand in as aligned a posture as you are able. Breathe. Let this sense of alignment become a template for the truth of your life.

STRENGTH

Strength is the ability to withstand force or pressure. It's the ability to bear things without buckling or breaking.

It's important to remember that strength also includes flexibility and resilience. If we become brittle, and hunker down too hard, we can get shoved over or snapped in two. Even in throwing a punch or kick, yes, we need dynamic tension to carry the force of the blow, but if we tense up too much, the blow weakens and we get hurt. The same is true for hammering in a nail. We need presence and accuracy, not simple brute force, to drive the nail home.

In other words, we need the ability to give and move in our strength, which works with our power, or our ability to do. Strength is capacity.

Flexibility and resilience both increase strength, and strength increases flexibility and resilience, if we allow it to. Think of the ways in which you face challenges or adversity. Do

PART III: AUTONOMY AND WILL

you tense up? Do you collapse? Do you draw upon your strength and flexibility?

Trees root more deeply to resist the wind. Plants root more deeply to find water. If there is no wind, or if water is always available near the surface, when adversity comes in the face of a storm or dry, hot wind, the trees will fall and the plants be uprooted.

We are the same. Using resistance increases our strength, physically, emotionally, and mentally.

This is not to repeat the old Nietzsche quote, *"What doesn't kill me, makes me stronger,"* because that is not always true.

Too much adversity and challenge is just has harmful to our strength as too little. Too much adversity can break us before we can gather enough strength to save ourselves or resist.

Nonetheless, strength lends stability and stability lends strength.

In our process of making commitments and showing up for what is important to us, we must comprehend our personal capacity to withstand force or pressure.

In life, sometimes we need to resist things. Other times, resistance becomes damaging. If we resist too much, we don't let enough in.

Sometimes, we undermine our own strength. For example, when we feel overwhelmed, like there is too much to bear in the world—and there is a lot—do we take a step back, take a break, and ask what might soothe our souls enough to recover? Or do we keep going, pushing, and punching constantly, wearing ourselves out? Or do we engage in hours of self-numbing behavior, until it becomes difficult to face our responsibilities and commitments again? Too much self-numbing activity only serves to weaken us, long term.

We need to assess when to push and when to back off. When to soothe ourselves and when to show up and try.

Like with our muscles, we need rest in order to grow stronger over time. Also like our muscles do, we need to engage with life in order to grow strong.

Strength, in this way, requires some patience. Building takes time.

PRACTICE:

Answer the following questions as best you can:

What strengthens me? What breaks me? Do I feel easily shattered? Overextended?

What nurtures and supports me? What helps increase my sense of strength? Is it exercise? Daily spiritual practice? Time with friends? Listening to music? Gratitude practice?

What is my current capacity? How strong do I feel today?

CULTIVATING STRENGTH

How can we practice strength?

Practicing strength is not the same as *"fake it 'til you make it."* To practice strength is to exercise the muscle of our will to show up, commit, and honor those commitments.

If we look at our lives, we'll likely find several ways we can increase our dedication, shift our inertia, and exercise our will.

We can examine all the facets of our lives by going through a checklist of assessment. We can look at our thought patterns,

PART III: AUTONOMY AND WILL

our emotions, our physical health and well-being, our sense of spiritual connection, our family and community systems, our work systems....

Work systems are a thing I'm often reassessing and pushing or softening my edges around. I challenge myself to examine which of my work systems actually support my larger project in the world and which no longer work for me depending on my current capacity. I look for things I can learn or study, and also assess when studying gets in the way of doing.

I do all of this so I can remain in the flow of my calling.

We can set an alarm for fifteen minutes earlier than usual so we can do some mediation or prayer before starting the rest of our day.

This spiritually trains us, helps re-set our nervous system, and trains our minds to center first, before the influx of activities or outside stimulation.

We can commit to a daily walk, or weight lifting, or stretching. To begin this sort of commitment can be as simple as saying, "I'll do ten countertop pushups while waiting for my tea water to boil."

This physically trains us, but also trains various parts of our psyche to say, "I can do this. I can grow stronger for myself, my community, and my life."

We can commit to slowing down and listening more attentively to children, or a partner, or our friends.

This lets us know we can increase our capacity for presence and attention.

We might study something that is challenging, enlisting our friends to study with us.

Perhaps we'll take a risk, and do something that we've wanted to do, but been afraid to.

We can contact a local organizer and ask how we can best hook into their project.

Perhaps we'll commit to turning off the show earlier, or not working late, so we can get more sleep.

We can make an appointment with a therapist so we have support in increasing emotional strength and resilience. Or maybe we need some healing work before we even begin to increase our emotional strength.

This list is by no means exhaustive. I just wanted to show a variety of small ways in which we can bolster will and increase our strength.

Following up on any of these small commitments strengthens our confidence. This practice teaches us that we can bring more to all of our commitments, large or small. The more we practice strengthening our will, the better the life we are called to lead is supported.

The smallest changes, diligently practiced, can yield large results.

The whole scope of our lives can either undermine or support us in living with greater strength and integrity. The challenge, then, is to look at our lives, and commit to our strength.

We begin by asking, "What is my current capacity, and what is the capacity I desire?"

In what ways might you challenge yourself to increase your strength?

. . .

PRACTICE:

Take a look, on the most basic level, at your life right now. Not the life you once had. Not the life you want. Your life, in this window of time.

Make a list: here are the activities and attitudes that help increase my strength.

Make a second list: here are the activities, patterns, and attitudes that diminish my strength.

Then, pick three things you can do to increase your strength.

STRENGTH AND COMMITMENT

How do we bring more strength to our commitments?

How do our commitments bolster our strength?

One example of this from my own life is my writing. I used to have to make a very strong commitment to logging a certain word count per day, in order to consistently get my butt in the chair. That took effort, concentration, and showing up. I even did sigil magic to focus my efforts. But mostly? I just kept practicing. Some days I didn't make that word count goal. That was fine. I would sit at my desk the next day, re-set my intention, and then I would practice.

In other words, I would write.

Now, I can often write that early word count goal in one hour. That also takes diligence, intention, and commitment. And I still use support systems, like setting a timer for twenty minutes and writing continuously until the timer goes off. Then, after a five-minute break, I begin again.

This gets my words flowing and, piece by piece, the story emerges.

Because of that early commitment, my writing practice is stronger now. I have greater capacity. People often ask how I am so prolific. My answer is that I strengthened my commitment to practice, and did not give up.

In this way, I bring my strength to my commitment to write. But my commitment was the impetus to increase my strength.

Without committing first, I would not have bothered to follow through. I'd likely still have half-finished novels languishing somewhere, the way I did decades ago, back when I noodled around, but never fully committed, despite saying I wanted to. I was waiting for something to change. Subconsciously, perhaps I was waiting to become strong.

All of that changed ten years ago, when I finally made a commitment, and then began to slowly work at increasing my capacity and my strength.

So now, what was very challenging has become relatively easy and simple.

I have other challenges now that I need to face, commit to, and learn, putting in time and effort to build those muscles.

But, since I've done it before, in many different ways, I know I can do so again, and even know what sort of strategies might help me.

What I'm talking about is the same when figuring out how to be of service after my family moved from California to Oregon. I had been deeply enmeshed in communities in Berkeley, Oakland, and San Francisco. I knew who needed help, how to show up and plug in, which group did what sort of justice work. I knew who was fighting the fight I wished to support.

After my move, I cast about, looked around, and tried some things. But nothing felt like the right fit. I had entered a different ecosystem. So, what did I do? I just started showing up. Slowly, I began to make contacts. I began to figure out how I could be of help.

This enables me to assess my life as it is now, and offer the sort of work and resources I can.

My strength has shifted, and I'm no longer able to honor my commitments in the way I could a decade ago. And that is okay. I have different strengths. Honoring that helps me choose the commitments that can both use my current strengths and help me increase in strength over time.

PRACTICE:

What is your current strength level? What is your current capacity?

In what ways are you willing to commit, in order to increase your strength? Pick one area of your life you'd like to bring your willingness to bear on. Then commit. Then practice. See how much your strength increases.

STRENGTH AND RESISTANCE

I wrote a little bit about resistance in the opening section of this chapter, but feel the need to revisit that.

There is the resistance the world itself offers us, from outside. The chafing of life rubbing against our edges. The detours or obstacles placed in our way. Sometimes this sort of outside resistance or pressure is something we can work with, or around, or even challenge and overcome. That increases the strength of our ability to say "yes" to ourselves and our practice.

Other times, we must listen to these obstacles and let our intuition assess whether or not the universe is trying to tell us something. In those cases, sometimes outside resistance helps us strengthen our ability to choose, or to set boundaries and say "no."

But now I want to examine internal resistance. This often arises from our current comfort levels, our inertia, or our insecurities and fears. We can come up with one hundred excuses for why we need to give in to this inner resistance.

For example, some days I have a "don't wanna" regarding creativity. Or business. Or going for a walk.

Excuses abound. It's too hot. Or I didn't get enough sleep. Or allergies are kicking my ass. Or my brain is foggy because of autoimmune issues....

Navigating that last factor, plus a touchy brain, means that I do actually need to monitor whether I need a day off or not. I've had to learn how to tell whether I need a break or need to try. Now, if I decide to try, and my brain completely wipes itself and says "nope," then that's a pretty clear sign that pushing through will only make things worse and create a situation of diminishing returns.

Usually, when I listen to resistance on days like that, and actually take a day off, the following day I return and am able to do all the things. Phew!

But what about the times where the "don't wanna"

PART III: AUTONOMY AND WILL

happens several days in a row? I lace up my sneakers or pull on my boots, and I go for that walk. I don't set a time, I just walk. Some days that means I'll start to feel better a few blocks in and go for thirty minutes or more. Other days? They're what—at my sickest—I used to call "dragging my carcass around the block" days. I'll walk for ten minutes or so and that's enough.

It's the same with writing. I occasionally have days where the "don't wanna" is strong. This is usually my critical brain acting up, nervous that my subconscious won't work things out, even though it always does.

So, what do I do when I'm feeling this sort of resistance?

I fall back on the advice from one of my writing mentors: *"Write the next sentence."*

Writing the next sentence is the same as pulling on my boots or lacing up my sneakers. Writing the next sentence is the equivalent to getting into a meditation posture. The posture itself reminds us of why we meditate.

It's the same with basic physical exercise: we show up, move our body, get some lymph flowing, release a few endorphins, and often find we're actually enjoying it. Even if it's just a little bit.

Back when I was working with a personal trainer, he remarked that he could always tell when my mind decided to give up. And my mind always gave up before my body did. I was convinced I had to give up. That I couldn't do it. That's where the encouragement from the trainer helped me do the next rep.

Back when I started what I usually just call sitting practice —because the word meditation can carry its own baggage and false expectations—I would set a timer and a bunch of parts of self that liked to stay in hiding began to squirm. If I could breathe with those parts long enough, eventually just the posture and the commitment to sit would cause those parts to calm down.

Internal resistance means always confronting parts of ourselves that want to run away, do it right, or hide in the shadows.

What would happen if we picked up the paintbrush or guitar? Or put on some music? Or wrote the next sentence?

By taking that first, simple action, we open to possibility. We strengthen our will, and our ability to show up and commit.

And in opening to possibility, new things arise.

Practice:

Below is a prayer I wrote several years ago. If it is useful, please feel free to use it yourself. If you say it every day, who knows what will happen?

A PRAYER FOR STRENGTH

Expand my capacity to heal.
    Expand my capacity to be of help.
    Expand my capacity to deeply rest.
    Expand my capacity to work for the greater good.
    Expand my compassion.
    Expand the breath, rising in my lungs.
    Expand my ability to love.
    Expand my discernment.

PART III: AUTONOMY AND WILL

Strengthen my ability to set boundaries.
Strengthen my ability to show up when needed.
Strengthen my ability to share what is good.
Strengthen my ability to listen well.
Strengthen my ability to speak the truth.
Strengthen my capacity to work with others.
Strengthen my heart.
Strengthen my mind.
Strengthen my gifts.
Soften my capacity to simply be,
In love with this world.
Right. Now.

COMPASSION

Compassion is the willingness to help relieve suffering. In this way, it is different from its close cousins, sympathy and empathy.

Sympathy can connect us to one another, but it neither acts nor feels. Mostly what sympathy does is express our sadness. Sympathy says, "I feel for you," though we do not fully comprehend the other person's feelings. With empathy, we actually *feel* your feelings. Or think we do. Both sympathy and empathy can be powerful expressions of human emotion, searching for kindness and connection in an often hostile world.

Compassion goes further than either of these. It doesn't have the remove of sympathy, nor does it need to directly experience emotional suffering in order to want to help.

Where empathy feels, and sympathy expresses sorrow, compassion acts. None of these qualities are better than another. Some of us are wired more toward sympathy, and some toward empathy. Other times it is situational.

For example, we may be more empathetic toward a person living through something similar to what we have lived through. But we can by sympathetic toward someone who's situation is radically different from ours.

The development of either sympathy or empathy can help us cultivate deeper compassion. Experiencing sympathy or empathy can instill in us a willingness to show up and help relieve suffering in whatever way we can. Remember, compassion acts, and for me, that ability holds great power and opportunity.

Compassion is where will and heart work together, strengthened, living with honor and truth, committed.

Self-compassion can help us navigate or surmount difficult personal obstacles. Giving ourselves grace instead of punishment, denial, or giving up strengthens us over time.

Similarly, compassion also serves our larger life commitments. If we have a commitment to a community, task, or the world, then compassion must enter. Otherwise, our commitments and strength can go down the road of brittleness, greed, or selfishness. We don't want that. Or, at least, I hope not!

We grow our capacity for compassion over time, by returning again and again to an open heart, engaged will, and a measure of grace.

How do we foster relationships?

We can consciously foster relationship with our meditation practice. Our physical practice. With our family. Our community. With the larger world. Our environment. Trees, flowers, insects, animals. Other human communities. The cosmos.

Fostering relationship with all of these helps open us to compassion.

Practice:

Do some writing, walking, or meditating around the following questions:

What are your current primary relationships? What would you like those primary relationships to be?

To work? A partner? A garden? A cause? Creative expression? Physical or mental health?

Once you've done some work with the above questions, take a breath. Drop into your body and exhale.

How can you bring compassion to each of these primary relationships? And how can you bring more compassion to your relationship with yourself?

COMPASSION AND HEART

Notice the connection between strength and compassion. Without compassion, we find, strength is nothing.

Without compassion, strength can easily twist into brutality. We see the effects of brutality globally. Some of us see the effects of brutality closer to home.

Strength without compassion becomes brittle or brutal. Instead, we want a flexible, resilient strength that can adapt to various situations. We want compassion to flow back to our initial commitment.

Compassion helps keep me on track. It reminds me why I'm doing what I'm doing. Why I'm showing up. I can't just be driven to accomplish a series of goals unwedded and unmoored from compassion, connection, and relationship.

Compassion reminds me *why* I am doing whatever it is, or in a relationship with the person, situation, or task. Without

PART III: AUTONOMY AND WILL

that why, we can too easily spend our efforts on things that do not really serve us, each other, or this earth. By linking compassion back to my commitments, I understand why I made that commitment in the first place.

Without that solid why, it is easy to just keep doing what we're doing, losing effectiveness, and eroding the connection with our reason for being and doing.

When we look at our lives through the lens of compassion, we gain more clarity.

Our lives and work are helped by looking at all the ways strength and compassion work together. And the ways honor and compassion work together. And truth and compassion.

Some of us may have too open a heart, and feel too much sympathy, empathy, or compassion. Sometimes we even tip over into pity. Pity is also unhelpful. Pity is not linked with strength. Pity tries to coddle people. Pity devalues and disrespects other people.

Self-pity devalues and disrespects us and our commitments and tasks. If I am stuck in self-pity, I am devaluing and undermining myself, my capacity, and my abilities.

If we find ourselves in self-pitying cycles, or pitying others, we can pause, take a breath, and ask: "In what way am I disrespecting or devaluing myself, this person, or this situation?"

Then we can ask how we can bring strength and compassion to the table instead.

Compassion breaks the cycles of both pity and punishment.

Compassion moves us forward, bolstering our commitments, and increasing our presence, resilience, and adaptability.

. . .

PRACTICE:

For this meditation, it will be helpful to have a cup or chalice filled with clear water.

What fills you with horror, or shame, or pity, or rage, or disgust? What would you like to hide from in yourself or in others? Gently wash your hands over your heart space, letting your fingertips glide over your breastbone.

Now fill your cup and gaze into it. Imagine that this cup is your emotional heart. What is in your heart? Can you love it? Can you look upon your heart with fierce tenderness? Breathe through your heart. Fill with compassion. Drink.

COMPASSIONATE INTEGRATION

Compassion helps us become more accountable.

Compassion can also work with anger, love, strength, joy, and honor. Compassion can be brought to bear on any situation, if we choose it.

The connective energy of our life flows from strength into compassion. The stronger and more integrated we become, the more we have access to compassion. A strong person is able to accurately act from empathy and mercy. The stronger we are, the less we pity others. The more integrated we become, the less prone we are to stalling out when things get tough, or even when we fall down.

Compassion reminds us that mistakes are made, and are actually necessary for our growth. Compassion for process helps us let go of the small stuff and keeps us on our path.

Lack of compassion is a sign of weakness, constriction, and scarcity. Compassion sees someone or some situation as they

PART III: AUTONOMY AND WILL

or it really is. As we touched upon in the previous section, this is not pity or coddling of weakness.

True compassion is the deepest respect, a form of seeing clearly that calls upon truth, strength, and honor. This compassion must be trained upon ourselves as well as upon others. Compassion also breeds generosity, more of the openness given by strength.

When we lack compassion for ourselves, it can become more difficult still to dredge up compassion for others, particularly those far removed from our experience. But in calling upon our commitment, honor, truth, and strength, we can remember that compassion brings more life force and depth of understanding than rejection does.

We do not have to countenance bad behavior, but keeping sight of the full humanity of the perpetrators will help us to balance our responses and therefore, rebalance the world.

We can be compassionate and angry. We can be compassionate and hold boundaries. We can be compassionate and hold others accountable.

Opening to compassion connects us to the full panoply of the world, in all of its beauty and pain.

A continued invocation of compassion exercises heart and mind, enabling us to be of greater service.

Compassion helps us to commit to the things that are important to us, and keep committing to action for the long haul. Even as things change.

ON BEING WITH

Compassion is about learning to be with. Sharing suffering. Sharing passion. Sharing experience.

Compassion does not barrel in and say: "I know the fix. I have the answer. Do this. Do that. Do this other thing. Let's go!"

I've had to learn this the hard way, because I tend to be a fixer, and I do think I know all the time, and sometimes I do. But I acknowledge that I can know better, deeper, and more appropriately if I pause and remember that I want to be with. I want to be with this person or this situation first.

Sometimes, we call this process "holding space." Or making space. Allowing space means we can enter into relationship and simply be *with* in that space. With a strong center, will, and heart, we can better assess any situation. We can ask questions. We cultivate the ability to be and feel and sense. This helps us deepen our compassion and understanding. This also helps us to connect more deeply so when it is right, we can show up, and have a fruitful, rather than damaging impact.

Being with is not blowing in like a tornado. Being with brings presence first, then assessment, and finally, the comprehension of what we can truly offer.

We need compassion for ourselves in order to comprehend what our abilities, skills, and capacities actually are. And we need compassion for the other person or situation, to see where we can best fit and be in relationship.

To reiterate: Compassion is not about fixing. Compassion is about being with.

. . .

PRACTICE:

What is your tendency? Are you a fixer? An avoider? Think of a recent situation, or an old situation that has stuck with you. Do you feel you handled the situation cleanly and clearly? Does something bother you about it? Was your impulse to fix or avoid or something else?

Just notice whatever comes up, and breathe with it. Remember, these are just tendencies. Impulses. Depending on how early they were entrained into us, these impulses may never go away, no matter how much we may want them to.

In noticing, we can turn compassion toward ourselves and breathe. We can practice patience or courage, deep listening or sensing. We can practice being with a person, situation, or task, no matter how much parts of us may want to fix or avoid.

Breathe with your impulses and tendencies. Make more space for being, in the midst of it all.

COMPASSION FOR THE LONG HAUL

One of the best ways I've found to build a sustainable relationship with compassion is to work on my boundaries.

I was trained into codependent behavior as a very small child. As a result, it took me many years to cultivate better boundaries. At each phase in my life, I need to revisit boundary work, always finding situations in which my boundaries were lacking, or failed me. For me, this happens most often when emotions run high, I sense injustice, or there is something that just *needs to be fixed.*

Poor boundaries look different for each of us. For some, it is getting involved in everyone else's business. For others, it is trying to fix things that are not ours to fix. For some of us, it is getting overtaken by strong emotions and losing our center. And others of us try to control people or situations outside ourselves in order to feel safe.

Others of us cut off people or conversations and name that a boundary when…it may be a healthy boundary, or it may be giving up out of fear of conflict, deep anger, or vulnerable exposure.

There are many other examples, too, and I'm sure you have seen or experienced plenty of your own.

So, how about you? What are your boundaries like? What helps you set healthy boundaries? Do you even know what those look like?

Why am I speaking of boundaries here? Without healthy boundaries, it is easy for compassion to devolve into the punishment or pity we touched on before. Without healthy boundaries, it becomes more difficult to recognize what the work is that will bolster my commitments and what is not my responsibility at all.

Remember our work with passion and wisdom. Arising from the power of water, both passion and wisdom engage with boundary and flow. Riverbanks. The walls of a cup.

Having a container for our compassion enables us to be more open-hearted and present in the moment.

Having a container for compassion helps us to live more compassionately long term.

Compassion with no center and no circumference too easily becomes pity, or coddling, or contributes to overreach and burnout.

If we find ourselves consistently returning to states of pity, overwhelm, or burnout, that is a sign to return to our centers, breathe, and let go.

After we let go for a while, we can regroup, reassess our commitments, and set new boundaries.

Then we can open out into compassion, once again.

This work is a cycle, and we continue to learn each portion of the way.

PRACTICE:

Breathe. Practice being in your center and noticing your boundary or circumference. I like to imagine my center as resting somewhere between my navel and pelvis, in my physical body. My circumference is the edge of the energetic field around my physical body.

I inhale, and drop into my center. I exhale out to my edges.

Do that for a few moments, then pull out your journal and answer these questions:

How can I practice bringing compassion to my commitments?

What happens when compassion and honor meet in me?

What light does truth bring to my sense of compassion? What light does compassion bring to my truth?

Where in me do strength and compassion meet? How can I better cultivate this?

Feel free to pull cards or runes for any of these, as well, or find images that reflect your answers.

THE CYCLE CONTINUES

All the points of this pentacle are interconnect—Commitment, Honor, Truth, Strength, Compassion—and altogether continuously form integrity and honor. They all strengthen us, help us live in our truth, and open us to greater compassion.

Feel all of these connections within your body, heart, and mind. Feel the ways in which those lines of connection feed and bolster each point. Here, you can also notice which lines feel weak or strong.

Breathe.

Let the lines connecting the points in the star shape help cleanse and activate the energies within.

Next, allow the sunwise circle to activate those qualities, and help us form healthier boundaries. As the sunwise circle turns along that outer edge, feel Commitment, Truth, Compassion, Honor, and Strength radiate out into the world.

Let us live our commitments truthfully. Let us bring

PART III: AUTONOMY AND WILL

compassion to that committed truth. Let compassion feed our honor and integrity. Bring that integrity to our strength. Allow strength to feed into commitment, once again.

In doing this work, we increase our ability to act effectively in this world, and in every realm of our lives.

CLOSING

I hope you have found the work here to be valuable. Over the course of several decades, these tools changed my life. My hope is that they will help you, in turn.

Feel free to go over the material in this book multiple times. Through exploration and repetition, the effects of these practices will change you, seeping into every cell, building you anew.

For me, the purpose of spiritual practice and magic has always been to help me to better assist others. The world is in need, be it to alleviate human suffering, environmental devastation, or to face any other crises. The more internal equilibrium we have, the better able we are to share power with one another.

Together, we can do our best to help the world.
Together, we can create more beauty and kindness.
Together, we can shine like the stars that we are.
Blessed be.

Acknowledgments

Thank you to all my students, teachers, and colleagues over the years, and to my Patreon supporters who read portions of this book as it was being written!

Thanks also to Bonnie Elizabeth for being such a great first reader, and Dayle Dermatis for editing.

And, as always, thank you to my chosen family. I could do none of this without you.

If you want to get weekly musings from Thorn in your inbox, or buy books directly from the author, please visit thorncoyle.com and thorncoylebooks.com
Also, reviews are always welcome!

About the Author

T. Thorn Coyle worked in many strange and diverse occupations before settling in to write books full time.

Author of the *Bookshop Witch Paranormal Cozy Mystery* series, the *Pride Street Paranormal Cozy Mysteries*, *The Steel Clan Saga*, *The Witches of Portland*, and *The Panther Chronicles*, Thorn's multiple non-fiction books include *Sigil Magic for Writers, Artists & Other Creatives*, *Kissing the Limitless*, *Make Magic of Your Life*, and *Evolutionary Witchcraft*. Thorn's work also appears in many anthologies, magazines, and collections.

An interloper to the Pacific Northwest U.S., Thorn drinks a lot of tea, pays proper tribute to the neighborhood cats, and talks to crows, squirrels, and trees.

Connect with Thorn:
www.thorncoyle.com

Also by T. Thorn Coyle

NON-FICTION

You Are the Spell Book and Oracle Deck

Sigil Magic for Writers, Artists, & Other Creatives

Crafting a Daily Practice

Evolutionary Witchcraft

Kissing the Limitless

Make Magic of Your Life

FICTION

The Witches of Portland

By Earth

By Flame

By Wind

By Sea

By Moon

By Sun

By Dusk

By Dark

By Witch's Mark

The Bookshop Witch Paranormal Cozy Mysteries

Bookshop Witch

Haunted Witch

Tarot Witch

Running Witch

Hallows Witch

Solstice Witch

The Pride Street Paranormal Cozy Mysteries

Sushi Scandal

Flower Frenzy

Muffin Murder

Hairspray Horror

Dandy Distress

The Mouse Thief

Mouse's Folly

Mouse's Fight

The Panther Chronicles

To Raise a Clenched Fist to the Sky

To Wrest Our Bodies From the Fire

To Drown This Fury in the Sea

To Stand With Power on This Ground

The Steel Clan Saga

We Seek No Kings

We Heed No Laws

We Ride at Night

Short Story Collections

A Hint of Faery

A Touch of Faery

A Spark of Magic

A Flame for Yuletide

A Hope for Winter

A Time for Magic

A Speculation of Stars

A Speculation of Hope

A Speculation of Time

Risk It All: Queer Stories of Love, Suspense, And Daring

Thresholds: Queer Stories of Love, Suspense, And Daring

Ghost Talker

Cats and Other Creatures

www.ingramcontent.com/pod-product-compliance
Lightning Source LLC
LaVergne TN
LVHW012249070526
838201LV00092B/164